SECRET
SOCIETIES...

AND HOW THEY AFFECT
OUR LIVES TODAY

OTHER BOOKS BY SYLVIA BROWNE

Adventures of a Psychic (with Antoinette May)
Astrology Through a Psychic's Eyes
Contacting Your Spirit Guide (book-with-CD)
Conversations with the Other Side
Exploring the Levels of Creation
If You Could See What I See
Meditations
Mother God
Secrets & Mysteries of the World
Spiritual Connections
Sylvia Browne's Book of Angels
Sylvia Browne's Lessons for Life

All of the above are available at your
local bookstore, or may be ordered by visiting:

Hay House UK: **www.hayhouse.co.uk**
Hay House USA: **www.hayhouse.com**®
Hay House Australia: **www.hayhouse.com.au**
Hay House South Africa: **www.hayhouse.co.za**
Hay House India: **www.hayhouse.co.in**

SECRET SOCIETIES...

And How They Affect Our Lives Today

Sylvia Browne

HAY HOUSE

Australia • Canada • Hong Kong
South Africa • United Kingdom • United States

First published and distributed in the United Kingdom by:
Hay House UK Ltd, 292B Kensal Rd, London W10 5BE.
Tel.: (44) 20 8962 1230; Fax: (44) 20 8962 1239. www.hayhouse.co.uk

Published and distributed in the United States of America by:
Hay House, Inc., PO Box 5100, Carlsbad, CA 92018-5100. Tel.: (1) 760 431
7695 or (800) 654 5126; Fax: (1) 760 431 6948 or (800) 650 5115.
www.hayhouse.com

Published and distributed in Australia by:
Hay House Australia Ltd, 18/36 Ralph St, Alexandria NSW 2015.
Tel.: (61) 2 9669 4299; Fax: (61) 2 9669 4144. www.hayhouse.com.au

Published and distributed in the Republic of South Africa by:
Hay House SA (Pty), Ltd, PO Box 990, Witkoppen 2068.
Tel./Fax: (27) 11 467 8904. www.hayhouse.co.za

Published and distributed in India by:
Hay House Publishers India, Muskaan Complex, Plot No.3, B-2, Vasant Kunj,
New Delhi – 110 070. Tel.: (91) 11 41761620; Fax: (91) 11 41761630.
www.hayhouse.co.in

Distributed in Canada by:
Raincoast, 9050 Shaughnessy St, Vancouver, BC V6P 6E5.
Tel.: (1) 604 323 7100; Fax: (1) 604 323 2600

A catalogue record for this book is available from the British Library.

ISBN 978-1-4019-1535-3

Printed and bound in Great Britain by TJ International, Padstow, Cornwall.

To Ben Isenhower,
for helping me sort through
the vast amount of research
for this book

CONTENTS

INTRODUCTION

*D*oing the legwork for my book *Secrets & Mysteries of the World* a few years ago led me down many eye-opening paths. I was especially intrigued, for instance, when I came across "secret societies" and their myriad influences and manipulations. Not only was I astonished by how much some of these associations have impacted human history, but I was downright flabbergasted when I realized that most people in this world of ours don't know that these organizations even exist. I was particularly astounded by the fact that many of the groups' own members have very little knowledge of their internal workings and innermost agendas.

As I researched the book you're currently holding in your hands, I couldn't believe how much has been written about secret societies yet how little is actually understood about them. I came to realize that this is because they're so often clandestine; after all, if a lot of information was openly available to you and me, such groups would no longer be operating in their preferred under-the-radar mode to fulfill their own agendas. But just what *are* the motives of these covert associations?

Most of us would logically deduce that if these organizations' purposes were for the betterment of humankind, then they wouldn't feel the need to be so cryptic. In fact, just the word *secret* tends to have negative connotations for us. In our minds, the term is the same as *hidden, mysterious,* and *unknown*—and is generally associated with lying, terrorism, and plotting who knows what against others. *Secret* also conjures up all sorts of other "bad things," such as cults, government cover-ups or covert operations, devil worship, spying and intelligence, and power- and money-mad syndicates that want to rule the world.

In other words, most of us don't like to have things withheld from us, and when we find that they have been, we're likely to become resentful. However, we also tend to then either ignore what we've discovered or become apathetic about it—and governments and religious organizations have been exploiting these common human traits for years. You see, a lack of information leads to disinterest and eventually acceptance . . . all it needs is time. How often has someone been all over the news, only to be forgotten several months later? We see this all the time with public figures in politics and the entertainment industry. Steroids in sports is a great example: The subject made big headlines at first, but now it's been relegated to the back pages of newspapers, as those in power have essentially made it go away.

No one who's trying to operate unseen craves attention or wants the general public to know what they're doing. That's why a book like Dan Brown's *The Da Vinci Code,* which focused on several secret societies, can be devastating to such organizations. While *The Da Vinci Code* is a work of fiction (with some fairly good research behind it), it was so well written and became such an international sensation that it's keeping these underground groups continually in the public eye. And now there are some nonfiction works coming out that are putting the world of these secret societies under a microscope to bring many truths to light . . . and that's where I come in.

What Francine Began

It seems that many of the books I've written originated from the work I've done over the 50-plus years I've been a professional psychic, teacher, and researcher. (My exploration has focused on many phases of human survival, as well as prophecies, religion, and trying to show what spirituality really is.) *Secret Societies . . . and How They Affect Our Lives Today* is no different—the members of my research group and I first came upon the topic innocently enough about 37 years ago, thanks to my spirit guide Francine. For those of you who don't know, Francine has been with me my entire life. Although I can hear her, I can't take listening to her for very long because her voice comes into my right ear and sounds really off-key. I therefore prefer to go into trance and have her speak *through* me to provide information for my research group.

Anyway, Francine had started out one particular session talking about the FBI during the reign of J. Edgar Hoover and how much he kept under wraps—that is, if he liked you or was bribed to keep silent—and then she went on to discuss secret societies. While even in those days we recorded, dated, and archived these trances for future reference, I wondered how on earth this information could ever be used because it seemed somewhat far-fetched and even a bit troubling. However, time has only proven that my spirit guide was actually rather accurate in what she told us.

For example, Francine offered some very grave predictions on the political side that I'm afraid are coming true even as we speak. Now please remember that this was around 1970—long before the onset of the Internet and a computer in every home—and she predicted that communications would be manipulated and affected in such a way that people could make bombs, regulate health care and transportation, and instigate wars. Someone in our research group asked why, and she simply responded, "For control, and to make a worldwide power." She also warned that what the United States had to offer could be matched by other nations, and maybe even done better. "Then," she warned, "it truly will become a fight over who gets to be the planet's power source."

Well, it seems that this has indeed come to pass, as we've seen in the areas of trade and technology, with more and more nations vying for global dominance. While everyone most likely started out with good intentions, as the power grew and governments gathered more money and workers, they've tended to become more corruptible. There can sometimes be a fine line between a benevolent leader and a tyrant; with increased competition for the world's resources, wealth, and authority, entire administrations can become compromised.

Francine also predicted the so-called oil shortage, saying that if you push people down far enough with fear, terrorism, transportation problems, economic messes, needless wars, and wasted natural resources, you'll get a complacent, defeated nation. And, my dear ones, what is America becoming now?

And not only did Francine pass along political bomb-shells almost four decades ago, but she also told us much of the information that went on to appear in books such as *The Da Vinci Code* and *Holy Blood, Holy Grail* years before they ever came out. You may wonder why I didn't impart what I knew then, and all I can say is that I can only do so much with my hectic schedule. There were other priorities that seemed much more important to me at the time. I was too busy with spiritual lessons; comforting people about what happens after death; helping individuals with their day-to-day lives; and writing and lecturing about dreams, angels, the Other Side, God, and so on. This all took precedence for me because I was trying to help as many men and women as I could . . . not just disseminating information that I felt would have a limited impact.

With the advent of all these works coming out about the relationship between Jesus Christ and Mary Magdalene, along with the secret societies that held that confidential knowledge about them, I guess I felt that it was finally time to set some things straight. I also wanted to give my readers some insight into what these covert associations really do and how they work and affect all of us. To that end, as we look at each of these groups, I hope that you'll make your own decision about them. If nothing else, they'll give you a fantastic window into human behavior!

What These Organizations Have in Common

Many of history's secret societies started out spiritually and attempted to keep it "pure"; others were just fraternal in nature or put together loosely, until they finally fell apart; while still others got into power, wealth, and politics. The one thing that they all had in common was banding together for a particular cause. The tragedy is that many of the organizations started out with the best and highest of intentions, which were then diluted down to base issues of greed, graft, and control.

Secret societies also share in the taking of oaths, along with penalties for breaking them. Depending upon the group, they'll take their oaths in one or more of the following categories, but as each association has vows that are specific to their needs, these are only a generalized overview:

- **The Oath of Secrecy:** Sometimes under penalty of death or excommunication, members not only pledge to keep all the secrets within the society, but often vow to give away money or other personal possessions.

- **The Oath Against Division:** Members promise not to deviate from the group's teachings or start their own organization based upon the one to which they've given an oath. They also vow to always work for the betterment of the society and not for themselves.

- **The Oath of Absolute Obedience:** Members pledge to absolutely obey the rules and order of the society. They must also pay homage to their headmaster or founder and often (but not always) follow the laws of the land.

- **The Oath of Honesty:** Members swear that they'll never tell a lie about anyone in the society or about the organization, and they promise to live within the group with honesty and forthrightness.

- **The Oath of Support:** Members vow to give support—morally, spiritually, or even financially—to the society. This can even extend to reporting any insidious conduct that would bring harm to the association.

Penalties

Discipline for breaking these oaths and other internal rules varies with each society and can run from being quite severe to members just having their hands slapped. Most punishments involve public humiliation by excommunication and being forever shunned by other members, having a person removed from power or position, or having a close friend in a lofty position removed from this seat of power.

Some penalties are so old and archaic that they're not actually enacted. For instance, it's been reported (but not proven) that the Shriners have a disciplinary action on their books that can result in their eyeballs being pierced and their feet flayed. In the very extreme, punishment can result in death to members and their families.

Other Commonalities

Almost all secret societies seem to pay homage to some kind of deity or honor, which ranges from God to the tenets of the group or its founder. And many members in religious organizations often pray that they're able to keep their pledges.

Aside from their own agendas, the majority of covert associations also contain some degree of what we might refer to as magic. I'm not talking about witches or sorcerers here, but rituals that initiate the individual into the group. For example, in the book *The International Encyclopedia of Secret Societies and Fraternal Orders,* Alan Axelrod states:

> Every generation recasts magic in its own likeness. To the Romans, famous for their once religious tolerance but frequently hard pressed politically, it was treated as any other political risk such as poisoning, murder, rebellion, and so on. To Christians, during their period of expansion, it was treated as a religious threat. Anything that did not fit into the norm of the world as it should be was "magic."

So many underground organizations have used so-called magical symbols steeped in mystery, which are merely tools to entice a new member with rituals, chants, incantations, and ceremonies involving pentagrams, the bones of dead bodies, and so forth—all used to prepare the initiate for acceptance into a group.

Even though some of the secret societies that are still around today had their beginnings after the time of Christ, Francine says that similar gatherings existed in ancient Rome, Egypt, Persia, Greece, and any other place where people felt that they couldn't live or worship as they wished. If there's one truth concerning secret societies, it's that there *is* no absolute truth because they differ in what they wish to accomplish. Whether they're political, religious or mystical, fraternal, or criminal, they all seem to feel the need to keep certain information from the general public—perhaps out of fear, for protection, or for some cause or agenda that they're dedicated to-which they believe is for the betterment of humankind.

Sometimes keeping secrets or belonging to a covert society makes individuals feel special, for they're sharing something that most people don't know anything about. As we take a closer look at these organizations, you'll also see how many of them put forth their truth under the guise of art, hiding clues within it to the very secrets they're protecting. In addition, I'll be giving you my take on much of this, as well as the information that Francine has provided over the years in research trances.

As the saying goes, when the student is ready, the teacher will appear. As your instructor for an intriguing subject, I've tried very hard to ensure that what I'm about to reveal in these pages is free from bias or without too much prejudice, but do know that it's *real.*

Politics vs. Religion

Most, if not all, secret societies can be tracked through valid investigation, although information about them will vary depending on how clandestine they really are. It's true that there aren't as many of these organizations today as there were in past centuries, and that certain periods of history seemed to have more of them than others. This is probably due to the current state of world affairs and everyday existence, as the harder life is and the less freedom is involved, the more covert groups seem to flourish.

As you're about to find out, while some of the most powerful have survived, hundreds more dispersed or just died out. Usually this happened because what the group was fighting for was only around for a short period of time, so when that era passed, the society dissipated; or the leader died and the others lost interest.

As I mentioned, some secret societies came into being before the time of Christ, but most of them arose during the Middle Ages, especially those associations that are tied into the mystical or religious genre. Many of these faith-based groups were products of the Crusades and the Catholic Church's unyielding stance about hiding the truth about Christ's birth and death, as well as the fact that he lived beyond the Crucifixion. You see, religions have their own agendas, and woe to anyone who stands in the way of their goals. The old adage of judging others by what they do rather than by what they say is particularly true here; in other words, if religious figures say to "love thy neighbor as thyself," but then go out and kill or commit atrocities against this same neighbor to advance their own agendas, they're certainly not doing the work of God.

So it turns out that what clandestine organizations have kept covered up are secrets dealing with religious dogma and those having to do with power and money.

(Unlike religious organizations, most of the political associations have only been around since the last century, thanks to the increasingly global nature of governments.) Years ago, church and state were combined and worked together to control an ignorant populace, and then they seemed to separate . . . but did they really? Today, while many of these covert groups fall into the political *or* religious domains, many of them span both arenas. For example, Freemasonry is a fraternal organization that has had a great impact in the political realm, yet it has many religious overtones as well.

In this book, I'll explain that many of these societies have similar agendas, to the point that experts feel that some of them have joined forces from time to time to advance their goals. I'll also show how many of these organizations have either used different monikers or changed their names altogether to avoid detection or persecution. (Suffice it to say that name changes don't really mean much except to the group trying to survive and preserve their secrets.) They've often disseminated false information to cover their tracks, or at the very least put up smoke screens to hide their activities. In addition, I'm going to point out that many of these clandestine associations are linked to conspiracy theories and actions that seem to advance their particular agendas in the long term.

The more you research secret societies, the more you'll find that in some small way they're all linked together, almost like different fingers of the same hand. Nevertheless, I decided to break up this book into three distinct parts. While there will be some overlapping among the groups, I'll be focusing on the political (Part I) and the religious (Part II) separately. Then in Part III, I'm going to take a close look at the dark side of all this secrecy—how fear and intimidation have been utilized by governments, religions, and underground organizations for centuries because they're so effective.

There are hundreds of covert groups, and by no means could I even hope to cover them all in one book. Rather, I tried to keep my focus on the ones that are either in the public eye or that might have a significant impact on society. (Also, since the amount of information on each organization varies greatly, some chapters will be significantly longer than others.)

Looking under these heavily guarded rocks shouldn't make you afraid; after all, knowledge is power. So welcome to the world of secret societies—get ready to find out what they've been trying so hard to hide for so many years.

PART I

POLITICAL
SOCIETIES

CHAPTER 1

SKULL AND BONES

*T*his famous organization has been designated as "America's secret establishment" by author Antony Sutton, but it's also been known as "the Brotherhood of Death," "the Order," or just plain "Bones."

For more than 150 years, Skull and Bones has been active at Yale University. Also called "Chapter 322," some claim that it's an offshoot of a secret German university society. This group allegedly had a fascist and communist bent, with a Hegelian philosophy of "service to the state." Many conspiracy theorists also believe that it was the infamous "Thule Society" (whose members went on to form the Nazi Party) and has ties with the Illuminati (which I'll discuss in Chapter 11).

Apparently, the American branch of this group was founded in 1832 at Yale University by class valedictorian William Russell and his schoolmate Alphonso Taft. William was the cousin of Samuel Russell, who made his fortune by smuggling opium to China, and he supposedly struck up a great friendship with a leader of a clandestine German university society during the two years he spent studying in Germany. He evidently became so enthralled that he got permission to form a branch in America.

William Russell later went on to become a state legislator in Connecticut and a military general. His partner, Alphonso Taft, was later appointed the United States' attorney general, secretary of war, and ambassador to both Austria-Hungary and Russia. Alphonso was also the father of William Howard Taft, who ultimately became the only man to be both chief justice of the Supreme Court and President of the United States.

Now, from what I've been able to gather from my research, Yale's chapter is the only one in America, although some say that there's also one at Virginia Commonwealth University in Richmond. Its members are known as "Bonesmen," "Knights of Eulogia," and "Boodle Boys," nicknames that are typical of college fraternal organizations . . . but this group seems to go beyond your average fraternity.

From a Tap to a President?

The identity of those who have been in Skull and Bones is assumed to be secret, but the group actually published membership lists (which were held in the Yale library) until 1970. Only after that time was membership kept secret. However, several leaks have occurred over the years—one of which was the result of a break-in, with another coming from a disgruntled member who gave a list of fellow Bonesmen to Antony Sutton in the mid-1980s. The membership reads like a who's who of East Coast society, with members from old, wealthy, and powerful families that are steeped in politics, banking, commerce, industry, and the like. Three Presidents of the United States (the aforementioned Taft, along with George H. W. Bush and George W. Bush) were Bonesmen, for instance; and the younger President Bush supposedly appointed 11 of his old "frat brothers" to his administration in his first term.

The way the initiation process works is that certain juniors at Yale are "tapped" (literally, on the body or shoulder) near the end of the school year to join the seniors-only society, resulting in about 15 new members being chosen. Although potential candidates can refuse membership, it's considered a great honor to be tapped.

Only males were eligible until 1992; through a secret referendum of existing members (which was purportedly quite heated), the group is now said to admit women. To be considered a candidate, it helps if you're from a Bones family; have access to wealth and power; and are energetic, active, political, and resourceful. To even be admitted to Yale in the first place requires academic prowess or familial influence, so the order can obviously pick from some of America's best.

Being a seniors-only type of association, one can basically assume that the goals of Skull and Bones probably have more to do with an agenda in the outside world than they do with Yale or "brotherhood." To that end, conspiracy theorists often have a field day with this group, tying it in with numerous other covert political organizations such as the Trilateral Commission, the Council on Foreign Relations, the Bilderberg Group, and the Illuminati (all of which I'll cover in this book).

Skull and Bones owns two pieces of property: their building on the Yale campus, called "the Tomb," which is actually quite large; and Deer Island, a private haven on the St. Lawrence River. Naturally, both locations are for the exclusive use of the order. The Tomb has no exterior windows, and its walls are made of concrete, even though it reportedly has many rooms (including several bedrooms). According to some who have been inside, there's a room devoted to William H. Taft and his Presidency that's almost like a shrine. And an eyewitness account of the inside of the Tomb by one of a group of Yale females invited for a tour by a "dissident" member claimed that there's another room that's apparently devoted to the Nazi regime in Germany, including quite a bit of "memorabilia." The witness is reported to have said the following:

> There were tons of rooms, a whole chain of them. They [sic] were a couple of bedrooms, and there was this monumental dining room with different rolls of Skull and Bones songs suspended from the ceiling. And there was a President Taft memorabilia room filled with flyers, posters, buttons—the whole room was like a Miss Havisham's shrine. And a big living room with a beautiful rug; and this big, huge, expensive-looking ivory carving in the hallway. The whole thing was on a very medieval scale. The most shocking thing—and I say this because I do think it's sort of important—I mean, President Bush does belong to Skull and Bones, everyone knows that—there is, like a little Nazi shrine inside. One room on the second floor has a bunch of swastikas, kind of an SS-macho-Nazi iconography. Somebody should ask President Bush about the swastikas in there. I mean, I don't think he'll say they're not there. I think he'll say, "Oh, it wasn't a big deal, it was just a little room." Which I don't think is true and which I wouldn't find terribly reassuring anyway. But

I don't think he'd deny it altogether, because it's true. I mean, I think the Nazi stuff was no more serious than all the bones that were around, but I still find it a little disconcerting.

Initiates to the order reportedly have to lie in a coffin naked and tell their sexual history to the other candidates—whether this is a harmless induction or for blackmail purposes, no one really knows. Initiates are also given names that they carry with them for the rest of their lives. For example, the younger President Bush's name is "Temporary" (make of that what you will).

In addition to Presidents, there have been at least 28 U.S. Senators or Congressmen who belonged to the order, including James Buckley, Prescott Bush, John Chaffee, Thomas Ashley, Jonathan Bingham, David Boren, Thruston Morton, Robert Taft, and John Kerry. Several other Bonesmen served as cabinet members in various administrations (such as William A. Harriman), and most of us know about George H. W. Bush's involvement with the CIA.

Some of the old-line American families that have ties to the order through the membership of one or more descendants include Whitney, Perkins, Stimson, Taft, Gilman, Wadsworth, Payne, Davidson, Pillsbury, Sloane, Weyerhaeuser, Harriman, Rockefeller, Lord, Brown, Bundy, Bush, and Phelps. Yes, those are the same names you see on brands all over the world, heading huge corporations in banking and industry and being leaders in the political arena. As you can see, membership in this club can mean rubbing elbows with the planet's elite.

Being a clandestine organization, Skull and Bones members take oaths that they won't reveal anything about the society or their affiliation with it. For example, both

George W. Bush and John Kerry refused to say a word about the order in recent interviews, and very few people list it on their biographical data. Since the group only accepts somewhere around 15 members a year, there are perhaps just 500 to 600 members alive at any given time, and most experts say that about a third of these individuals are active in working for the group. It's also postulated by many that these active members are deeply involved in politics and big business—some have even reportedly been tied to drug trafficking and various scandals such as Iran-Contra, Watergate, the JFK assassination, and nefarious dealings with China and the Soviet Union.

Whether you believe that Skull and Bones is a powerful secret society or just a typical college fraternal organization, there's no denying the fact that its members are extremely influential people, and they have impacted affairs all over the world. If you'd like to read more about the order, I recommend the following books:

- *Fleshing Out Skull & Bones: Investigations into America's Most Powerful Secret Society,* by Kris Millegan, et al.

- *America's Secret Establishment: An Introduction to the Order of Skull & Bones,* by Antony Sutton

- *Secrets of the Tomb: Skull and Bones, the Ivy League, and the Hidden Paths of Power,* by Alexandra Robbins

CHAPTER 2

~~~

THE COUNCIL ON FOREIGN RELATIONS

*T*he Council on Foreign Relations (CFR), which some
people regard as a think tank, describes itself as
being "dedicated to increasing America's understanding of the world and contributing ideas to U.S. Foreign
Policy. The Council accomplishes this mainly by promot-
ing constructive, closed debates and discussions, clarify-
ing world issues, and publishing [the magazine] *Foreign
Affairs*," (see their Website: **www.cfr.org**). Although that
statement seems innocuous enough, many think that the
CFR is perhaps the most powerful private organization to
influence American foreign policy, and that it's involved
in seeking a "New World Order" (a concept I'll discuss in
detail in Chapter 12) as well.

In his book *The Anglo-American Establishment*, Dr.
Carroll Quigley (mentor to President Clinton at George-
town University) claims that gold and diamond magnate
Cecil Rhodes formed a secret society called the "Society
of the Elect" in 1891 to, in Rhodes's words, "absorb the
wealth [and] take the government of the whole world."
Rhodes's covert association consisted of an inner "Circle
of Initiates," along with a larger collection of helpers

who formed "Round-Table Groups." These Round-Table Groups—along with members of the Fabian Society and a group called "the Inquiry," which was started by President Woodrow Wilson's chief advisor, Colonel Edward House—created the Royal Institute of International Affairs in Great Britain, and its American branch, the CFR, in 1921. Both CFR member Arthur Schlesinger, Jr. (in his book *A Thousand Days*) and Professor Quigley (in his book *Tragedy and Hope*) have referred to the CFR as a "front" for the power elite.

Quigley has always maintained that Rhodes scholarships were merely a façade to conceal Rhodes's secret society, as well as a training ground for those with the scholarships to gain the skills necessary to carry out his ultimate goal of world domination. It seems that this might indeed be the case; after all, many Rhodes scholars—including Walt Rostow, Dean Rusk, Richard Gardner, Harlan Cleveland, J. William Fulbright, George Stephanopoulos, Robert Reich, Ira Magaziner, James Woolsey, and Bill Clinton—have held high positions in American government. Some might say that Quigley's credibility is in doubt, but *The Washington Post* evidently felt that the information he obtained from "secret records" was valid when it published a 1975 article about him, titled "The Professor Who Knew Too Much."

Although my research indicates that Cecil Rhodes's conspiracy ended sometime around 1960, it apparently did so because it was no longer necessary. There were now enough "globalists" (proponents of a worldwide government) in place in politics, economics, education, and journalism to keep the power elite happy in their pursuit of a New World Order.

Part of this process was a plan started by William C. Whitney (a past member of Skull and Bones) and others to control America's political parties through financial contributions. Their original idea was to have the major parties alternate control of the government so that the public would think they had a choice come Election Day. This eventually evolved into having the power elite move both parties toward the political center. This resulted in the Democratic and Republican parties becoming almost identical in nature so that even if the American people did "throw the rascals out" in any election, it wouldn't lead to any major shifts in policy.

It's amazing to see how many members of government, education, the military, industry, and the media have affiliations with Skull and Bones, CFR, Rhodes scholarships, and the Trilateral Commission (which I'll be covering in the next chapter). All of these groups seem to have a globalist goal, and it certainly looks as if they have the people in place to speed that agenda forward. CFR membership is made up of present and past U.S. Presidents, ambassadors, secretaries of state, Wall Street investors, bankers, foundation executives, think-tank leaders, lobbyist lawyers, military officers, industrialists, media owners and executives, university presidents and key professors, select members of Congress, Supreme Court justices, federal judges, and wealthy entrepreneurs. It seems that they have all of their bases pretty well covered, especially when many people in foreign governments and other heads of state are also involved with the CFR in sister organizations (such as the aforementioned Royal Institute of International Affairs).

There are some who say that the CFR isn't actually a secret society because it files an annual report, publishes a magazine, and furnishes a list of its members to the public. That's all true . . . but they also make it a condition of membership that no one who joins may disclose what goes on or is discussed in their meetings. They have regular confidential gatherings and then once in a while hold a public conference and invite the press, thus making it appear as though they're just a harmless group with an agenda to help America.

In alphabetical order, here are a few of the more notable CFR members, along with their roles in the American power elite as of this writing:

- Richard V. Allen (former national security advisor)

- John Bolton (former ambassador to the United Nations)

- William F. Buckley, Jr. (founder of *National Review*)

- George H. W. Bush (former President and CIA director)

- Jimmy Carter (former President)

- Dick Cheney (current vice president)

- Bill Clinton (former President; current member of the Trilateral Commission and the Bilderberg Group)

- John Edwards (former senator from North Carolina)

- Dwight D. Eisenhower (former President)

- Anne Garrels (current correspondent for National Public Radio)

- Timothy F. Geithner (current president of the Federal Reserve Bank of New York)

- Newt Gingrich (former Speaker of the House of Representatives)

- Alan Greenspan (former chairman of the board of governors of the Federal Reserve)

- Katherine Harris (former representative from Florida)

- Herbert Hoover (former President)

- Jack Kemp (former representative from New York)

- John Kerry (current senator from Massachusetts)

- Henry Kissinger (former national security advisor and secretary of state; current member of the Trilateral Commission and the Bilderberg Group)

- Lyman Lemnitzer (former chairman of the joint chiefs of staff)

- Robert S. McNamara (former secretary of defense and president of the World Bank)

- Richard Nixon (former President)

- Colin Powell (former secretary of state)

- Dan Rather (former *CBS Evening News* anchor)

- Condoleezza Rice (current secretary of state; former national security advisor)

- David Rockefeller (former chairman of the Trilateral Commission and member of the Bilderberg Group)

- Donald Rumsfeld (former secretary of defense)

- Paul Wolfowitz (former deputy secretary of defense; current president of the World Bank)

There are many more individuals who could be mentioned here, but I just wanted to show you how much power, wealth, and influence is contained in CFR membership, especially when you factor in that some of these men and women also belong to Skull and Bones, the Trilateral Commission, and the Bilderberg Group. Now some will say that these leaders of America are all merely good friends who just happen to be a part of the same organizations, but I don't see them all belonging to the YMCA, do you? I've found that where there's smoke, there's fire . . . so it's no wonder that conspiracy theorists are screaming at the tops of their lungs about this blazing inferno.

In fact, none other than the famous author H. G. Wells exposed this secret society and its goals. You see, Wells was a member of the Fabian Society (a British socialist intellectual movement), abruptly quitting when they wouldn't make their goals (which he agreed with) public. Wells wrote several books outlining what he called "the open conspiracy," including *New Worlds for Old; The Open Conspiracy: Blueprints for a World Revolution;* and *The New World Order*—all of which I recommend that you check out.

CHAPTER 3

THE TRILATERAL COMMISSION

*W*hen you talk about modern covert political organizations, one name is on the lips of almost every conspiracy theorist out there: David Rockefeller. Now guess whose brainchild the Trilateral Commission (TC) was. Yep, you got it.

Mr. Rockefeller was 92 years of age in June 2007 and is reportedly the 215th wealthiest person in the world. He's been intensely involved with the Council on Foreign Relations (CFR) and the Bilderberg Group (BG), and he formed the TC in 1973 with Henry Kissinger and former National Security Advisor Zbigniew Brzezinski. This covert organization's membership consists of about 300 to 350 private citizens of Europe, Pacific Asia (Asia and Oceania), and North America, whose purported aim is to form closer cooperation between these three areas of the world.

Bill Clinton, George H. W. Bush, Jimmy Carter, Dick Cheney, and Senator Dianne Feinstein are either current or past members of the TC; and almost all of them also belong to the CFR. There are too many notable individuals to list here, but suffice it to say that there's a great deal of power and influence in the membership of the TC. To illustrate this, we only have to look at the election of Jimmy Carter as President of the United States.

Approximately seven months before the 1976 Democratic National Convention, a Gallup poll found that less than 4 percent of Democrats supported Mr. Carter for President . . . and then the TC took him under their wing. They mobilized the power and money of Wall Street bankers, the academic community, and the media controllers who were members of the CFR and the TC to try to get the governor of Georgia nominated. Almost overnight—and certainly out of the blue—Carter was indeed nominated and later became President. This example clearly proves how strong this group's power is. To that end, former senator and Presidential candidate Barry Goldwater once said, "[The TC] is intended to be the vehicle for multinational consolidation of the commercial and banking interests by seizing control of the political government of the United States." These may seem like strong words, until you realize that Mr. Goldwater was a staunch opponent of the CFR and David Rockefeller.

The TC meets annually in Europe, North America, or Asia; and its members (like those in the CFR) aren't permitted to say anything about the proceedings to the public. Like the CFR, the TC publishes a magazine, releases annual reports, and denies that it's a secret society. And while most conspiracy theorists believe that the CFR and the TC largely consist of individuals with good intent, these researchers point out that the inner circle is indeed obsessed with the agenda of getting a New World Order in place with one global government.

My research indicates that most of those who join the TC and the CFR are upright people. Yet it seems as if the higher echelon in these groups isn't telling all of their members exactly what's going on behind the scenes, and they're using their input to further their own agenda. I can't say that those in control are evil, because they may believe that what they're doing *is* for the betterment of the world.

It's a matter of opinion as to the dangers of a New World Order; certainly I believe that most Americans wouldn't want it to occur. If that's indeed the case, then we must be watchful and follow the actions of both the CFR and TC closely. After all, the more we know, the better prepared we'll be to either support *or* fight something. (Again, I'll be examining this subject more closely in Chapter 12.)

CHAPTER 4

THE BILDERBERG GROUP

*W*e're now going to take a look at another association that's been tied to both the Council on Foreign Relations (CFR) and the Trilateral Commission (TC), as well as the cause of globalization. The Bilderberg Group (BG) was initiated by Polish émigré and political advisor Joseph Retinger, who also served as its first permanent secretary; and its alleged aim was to promote a greater understanding between Europe and the United States.

The BG evidently got its name from the place of its first meeting, which occurred in May 1954 at the Hotel de Bilderberg in Oosterbeek (near Arnhem) in the Nether-lands. Today this organization gathers at an annual conference lasting four days at a five-star resort or hotel, usually in Europe, although several events have taken place in the United States and Canada.

While the BG isn't considered a club of any sort, many guests are regular attendees, and each year about 100 people are invited by a steering committee to attend the annual conference. Although these meetings aren't publicized, their times and locations, along with a list of attendees, *are* available for public knowledge. What's discussed within the conference, however, is *not* made known—and again, all members swear that they'll never divulge what transpires during these sessions, ostensibly because it ensures that no one will be misquoted. And even though some members of the media do attend, they're also required to keep mum about what takes place during the conferences. It's this secrecy that rings the alarm for conspiracy theorists.

Regular attendees include central bankers, defense experts, prime ministers, royalty, mass-media barons, government ministers, international financiers, and political leaders from Europe and America. Prominent guests have included Presidents Bill Clinton, George H. W. Bush, Gerald Ford, and Ronald Reagan, along with our old buddies David Rockefeller and Henry Kissinger, and numerous other TC and CFR members. Apparently the gang's all here!

I don't mean to sound overly suspicious, but it's interesting that the same people belong to these societies, all of which seem to share the globalization perspective of a one-world government. They also appear to groom new and talented members who always manage to climb the ladder into high positions in government, commerce, and industry. I'm sure that this is just the manifestation of the power elite—that is, if you're backed by them, you're almost guaranteed to attain a certain level of influence . . . as long as you remain true to their purpose.

The main thrust of the Council on Foreign Relations, the Trilateral Commission, and the Bilderberg Group feels like a form of regionalization, which in turn seems to be a step in creating a world under one government. I believe that most of the members of these organizations are good people without any real wicked intent and that some, especially those who really "pull the strings," probably have altruistic motives that tend to expand any power and wealth they may have.

However, I also realize that power can certainly corrupt, and that the concept of a New World Order will be very difficult to attain—especially since so many would be willing to die to retain their national identity—and I genuinely think that this goal won't come to fruition other than in pockets of regionalization for the purposes of defense and economy. One final warning here: If the United Nations continues to be given more and more power to intercede in world affairs, we all need to keep our eyes open.

CHAPTER 5

THE FREEMASONS

*O*ne of the most talked-about secret societies on the face of the planet has got to be Freemasonry, and the preponderance of books on the subject would choke the proverbial horse 20 times over. And it's not just the weighty tomes out there that make exploration daunting—there are also myriad ideas, theories, and histories that seem to spout off in every direction. In other words, my dear readers, there's a heck of a lot of information available about the Freemasons!

Before I started this chapter, I took one look at my floor, which was covered in research materials, and just shook my head, not really looking forward to delving into all this information. Here's a sample of the notes I took as I began my quest: *Ah, here we are . . . some work on the beginnings of Freemasonry. Let's see, this first book says they started in the early 17th century in Scotland. However, this other book claims they started in the 14th century, and still another states they started with the Knights Templar. So far I'm batting a thousand—three books and three different answers. Let's try another to see if we can come up with some consensus here. This paper says they started with the building of the Temple of Solomon and originated from an architect named Hiram. Yet another book* [I'm nothing if not persistent!] *insists that Freemasonry started with Adam. Who's next—God?*

I know I'm being a bit tongue in cheek here, but I've found that when a large amount of writing on a particular subject exists, that topic is invariably controversial and either loved or hated. The material that's out there on Freemasonry doesn't differ too much from the writings about other covert organizations, in that the group has its detractors and champions, along with the inevitable conspiracy plots—but there's just so much of it to wade through!

In fact, to call Freemasonry a clandestine group is probably a bit of a misnomer, particularly since in recent years members have stated that their organization is no longer so much a secret society as it is a society with secrets. I tend to agree with that assessment. With many former members putting out articles about Freemasons' rituals, it's a wonder that any of their mysteries are left at all. However, conspiracy theorists still have their field day with this group, and I don't see that changing too much. Whenever you have people holding meetings and conducting rituals in private, you're going to find someone who thinks that they're somehow plotting against the world.

Humankind has always been suspicious of anyone who does anything "under the radar," and that's how it should be. Such wariness helps keep a system of checks and balances in place, much like what the U.S. government has. (Whether those intended oversight mechanisms will continue to operate as they should in a world in which terrorism is running rampant remains to be seen, as many U.S. freedoms seem to be eroding . . . but that's a subject for another time.)

A Workers' Guild

As you can tell from my notes at the beginning of this chapter, the origins of Freemasonry are extremely unclear. There are as many hypotheses about this group's formation as there are scholars and historians, especially when myths and legends have gotten so mixed in with the facts.

Let's explore how Freemasons got their name. Most scholars can at least agree that three explanations are likeliest:

1. Early stonemasons were, by and large, free men. At one time, the various skills of masonry were at a premium because of the large number of churches, castles, and cathedrals that were being built. Masons and other craftsmen, unlike serfs and farmers, were allowed their freedom because they were proficient in the building trades and could travel around and find work at will. Hence, they became known as "free-men masons," which was then shortened to "freemasons."

2. Masons worked in freestone (a type of quarry stone) and were therefore "freestone masons," which again was shortened to "freemasons."

3. The final and most probable explanation comes from the French term *franc-macon,* which denoted a mason who'd been granted a contract by a church to work on its property, therefore being "free" from taxation or regulation by the king or local municipality.

One of the main traditions of Freemasonry arose when stonemasons would gather together to construct a large building. First they'd erect a "lodge" in which to house and feed the workers while they completed a project—depending on the time it took to finish the building, lodges ranged from temporary (a few months' work) to substantial and permanent (many *years'* work). These structures, which evolved into the modern-day Masonic temples, are the ruling centers of the Freemasons. (I'll talk more about lodges later in the chapter.)

History tells us that workers' guilds (the early unions) existed well before the time of Christ. They're mentioned in both Greek and Roman documentation, and my spirit guide Francine says that Freemasonry as we know it today actually started around A.D. 300. Now it's very interesting to note here that this time period coincides with the beginning of the Dark Ages, along with the recognition of Christianity by the Roman Empire.

Francine states that Freemasonry began as an added protection to ensure that workers employed by the Catholic Church would keep quiet about the centuries-old secrets they happened upon. She says that although the society didn't originate in Egypt, knowledge of ancient Egyptian and Persian mysteries was absorbed by masons who worked in those areas. While building their temples, mosques, and Coptic churches, these laborers became acquainted with many priests, architects, and scholars who possessed lots of hidden knowledge—including certain building secrets as well as other esoteric information—which was then passed on to fellow masons.

You must remember that although these were the Dark Ages for Europe, the Muslim world was flourishing and going through a golden age at the time, one in which science, the arts, and trade were making great strides. Consequently, Freemasonry became a workers' guild that also had access to several Middle Eastern mysteries, along with that region's great skill in the building arts. With the political and religious worlds entering into a state of flux, the craftsmen felt that it was prudent to confine their knowledge to themselves, thus forming a covert society of guild workers to do so. In addition to their building secrets, the esoteric knowledge they'd garnered was utilized to help form and shape bonds of closeness and fraternity.

A Nonreligious Brotherhood

There was a lot of diversity within the Freemasons due to their constant traveling, which was necessary so that they could build in different areas. Consequently, members came from several countries, ethnic backgrounds, and religions—they were a melting pot of stonemasons from various cultures thrown together out of necessity resulting from the overwhelming demand for their highly skilled work. This could very well have caused some trouble under normal circumstances, as it frequently did with other artisans' groups. Yet the advent of Freemasonry solved many of these concerns and made them just about the strongest of all the guilds.

Francine says that in Rome around A.D. 300, a group of masons working on local projects started to interact with each other over problems they were having. There had been several fights, and even a killing or two, due to some of the workers' cultural and religious differences. These altercations led to delays in construction, which meant lost time and wages. It also meant that the army had to get involved (you must remember that at this point in history, the Roman Empire was still in control). Since the social and religious climate was quite testy at the time—with a group calling themselves "Christians" creating a lot of havoc, and Roman borders being constantly assailed by uprisings—the soldiers weren't exactly gentle in their dealings with the troublemakers. This led to more injuries and lost time for the stonemasons . . . problems that were solved by forming their own covert organization.

According to Francine, all of the masons gathered together for a large meeting. Knowing that it would be human nature to sit with your friends or a clique based on some ethnic or religious background, the guild selected various members from each of these groups and put them together with the three top supervisors of labor to form a type of council, which was to come up with a solution for the problems that were occurring. Now all workers' guilds at that time had rules and regulations, just as unions do today—but in this case, instead of augmenting the existing rules, they set out on a different tack.

Francine says that it took a while, but they eventually were able to come up with a plan for a completely new organization. She explains that they realized that just the common "guild rules" weren't going to suffice, so they extended the purpose of the group to not only organizing the stonemasons, but to forming a brotherhood as well. She goes on to state that one of the first things they did was to incorporate that brotherhood by making it a nonreligious society that recognized a type of "universal creator" who could be accepted by any known religion. This meant that whether you worshipped Greek, Roman, Persian, Egyptian, or Far Eastern gods; Jehovah; or the new Lord of the Christians named Jesus Christ (Islam hadn't been founded yet), all would be welcomed under the same umbrella. This was an unfamiliar and ambitious concept for the time, and it emphasized religious tolerance.

In addition, Francine points out that the Freemasons took all of their knowledge from construction and the ancient mysteries of Persia and Egypt and put them into what we might call categories, much like the skill levels of "apprentice," "journeyman," and so forth that exist in trades today. Thus, they ensured that any member who desired to do so could advance through levels of knowledge just as they could through skill in their profession.

Francine claims that they topped everything off with pomp and ceremony by instigating rituals for each level of knowledge, as well as an initiation ceremony. They came up with symbols and titles to go along with these levels, bestowing a feeling of worth upon those who could õbtain certain levels of advancement. Utilizing the symbology and esoteric teachings of the cultures they'd worked for over the years, each level became an opportunity for gaining more knowledge, as well as raising one's morality and goodness. By doing so, a Freemason would then become a skilled worker *and* a more outstanding citizen. It was the hope of the group's "founding fathers" that this would help solve some of the problems that they'd been having in their local area. They had absolutely no idea how large their organization would become, or how great an impact it would have on the world.

Francine says that early Freemasonry was much more rudimentary than it is today; for example, there were fewer levels (or what they now call "degrees"), the ceremonies were neither elaborate nor long, and trappings were at a minimum. However, she notes that they did hold regular meetings to work out any difficulties and to instigate improvements when warranted, and that almost every stonemason in Rome joined this new organization.

Freemasons adopted an initial hierarchy based on knowledge and skill (which continues to this day), and as they left Rome for other areas of the world, they took with them their love for their newly founded society. As the brotherhood swiftly spread to other cities and countries, it became apparent that members needed a way to recognize one another; thus, a form of secret language through signs was instigated. They also realized that due to others' curiosity, they had to keep their knowledge, rituals, and basic organization as hidden as possible, so new oaths had to come into play.

The Roman Catholic Church was especially hard on those who had any form of religious tolerance or what they might deem to be blasphemous knowledge, causing early Freemasons to often be put between a rock and a hard place. You see, since many of the building projects were instigated and paid for by the Church, members had to balance their employers' wishes and their loyalty to Freemasonry. Combine this with the Church's paranoia and its zeal for ferreting out and punishing heretics, and you've got a recipe for a sticky situation.

Freemasons didn't see anything wrong with their organization, but the Church wasn't a forgiving entity and has clashed with Freemasonry in one way or another throughout its history. Just as it had done to countless other covert organizations, the Church forced the Freemasons to become more secretive to survive.

≈

Now I'd like to briefly touch upon the Freemasons' time with the Knights Templar. (I'll explore the Knights in detail in the next chapter.) While many people think that the Freemasons began with, or came out of, the Knights Templar, Francine says this isn't true. Yet the two groups did have considerable interaction because of the many building projects that the Templars hired stonemasons to work on.

The Templars used what they called "sacred geometry" in their architecture, part of which involved the construction of churches in the circular and polygonal patterns after the Dome of the Rock and the octagonal pattern of the Church of the Holy Sepulchre in Jerusalem. (Examples of such edifices are the Temple Church in London and the Chartres Cathedral in France.) However, most Templar structures were built in the local style of their particular locations. Some say that this was a cost-saving action, for as wealthy as the Templars were, they couldn't afford to give every single building they erected an expensive design.

It's estimated that beginning in 1170, more than 80 cathedrals and 500 abbeys were built in France alone due to Templar help or influence. The Freemasons were with them in all of these projects, and their partnership lasted until the essential demise of the Knights Templar in 1312. Francine is sure, as I am, that both groups had access to the truth about Christ (please see Chapter 14 for more on this), even though she says that Freemasons won't admit it today.

With the demise of the Knights Templar, Freemasonry went even deeper underground for a time in order to avoid getting caught up in what was then becoming an epidemic of paranoia on the part of the Catholic Church in its Inquisitions. In the 16th century, the Reformation came upon the scene, and the Catholics were too busy fighting the newly formed Protestants to be as vigilant about secret societies as it had been in the past—so Freemasonry was able to poke its head out into the open again. It wasn't until the latter portion of the 17th century, however, that Freemasonry really changed its course and started to become the organization that it is today.

Grand Lodges and a New Era

I want to stress here that the formation of a workers' guild doesn't necessarily make a society a secret one. We must remember that most people were very uneducated in the era of history we're focusing on here, especially in Europe. Artisans' groups formed to help their members make a living and support their families. *Survival* was the key operating word of the day.

Now, getting back to Freemasonry, we have to look at its evolution in two parts:

1. The early history of the group, in which it was confined to "craftsmen only"

2. The allowing of non-craftsmen to enter
   its ranks in the 17th century

These two time periods are like night and day, in that
we have a fraternal organization for skilled craftsmen
turning into what we might call an educated "gentlemen's club" virtually overnight. With those of the gen-
try now being let in, talk turned from construction to
philosophy and more philanthropic pursuits. There was
a type of reawakening, for all of a sudden there came an
influx of new members, many of whom started becoming
more and more fascinated with the ancient teachings of
their society that had been handed down for hundreds
of years.

Most scholars and historians believe that the heyday
of Freemasonry was in the 18th and 19th centuries . . .
and this is also the period in which conspiracy theorists
came out in droves to accuse the organization of almost
everything under the sun. Yet from all that I've been
able to gather, the change from a guild that was made up
exclusively of working (or "operative") stonemasons to
one in which anyone was allowed to enter started in the
Scottish lodges in the 17th century. The earliest record
of a nonoperative member attending a meeting was in
the Lodge of Edinburgh in June 1600, while the earliest
record of the initiation of a such a member was in July
1634 in that same lodge.

The first Grand Lodge in Freemasonry was founded
in 1717 in London, when four existing lodges met and
formed a larger one that encompassed them all under
the same jurisdiction. This would later go on to become
the "United Grand Lodge of England (UGLE)," but not

without some difficulties. For many years a number of other lodges in England refused to join this newly formed Grand Lodge and instead formed their own. These were often called "St. John's Lodges," and their members were called "ancients," "Old Masons," or "St. John Masons." They derisively called the first Grand Lodge the "moderns"; thus, you had a "moderns" Grand Lodge and an "ancients" Grand Lodge. The two finally merged in 1813 to become the Grand Lodge of England—considered to be the oldest Grand Lodge in existence, it put forth a type of Freemasonry that continues to be followed by the majority of members throughout the world.

The oldest jurisdiction in Europe is the "Grand Orient de France (GOdF)," which was founded in 1733. The GOdF was initially on good terms with the UGLE, but in 1877, a "great schism" developed when the GOdF decided to admit atheists as members (it already recognized women in Freemasonry). Since that time, except for minor "truce" periods, the two lodges have had no formal relations with each other.

Another French Grand Lodge, the "Grande Loge Nationale Française (GLNF)," is currently the only one in France that has formal relations with the UGLE. Because of this rift, Freemasonry today is said to consist of two different main branches:

1. The UGLE and concordant tradition of jurisdictions termed *Grand Lodges in amity*

2. The GOdF tradition of jurisdictions—often termed *Grand Orients in amity*

In most Latin America countries, the GOdF tradition

predominates (but almost all lodges maintain formal relations with UGLE), while in the rest of the world the UGLE tradition predominates with some minor variations.

In other words, all of Freemasonry is not always on the same page, which perhaps explains why there's no central organizational structure or authority. Although Grand Lodges have ruling jurisdictions that may include other Grand Lodges ruling a portion or section of their territory, there isn't one that's above all of the other lodges of Freemasonry. In fact, individual lodges have a large amount of autonomy over their own affairs, and the order prefers to keep it that way. Freemasonry seems to be made up of individual lodges that are under a particular Grand Lodge's jurisdiction, which then may or may not fall under the jurisdiction of another Grand Lodge itself.

Freemasonry is like a giant quilt, with little patches (individual lodges) making up squares (Grand Lodges), which in turn might make up a section (larger Grand Lodges)—yet no one Grand Lodge is the whole of the quilt (that is, no one entity rules over all). Apparently this works out quite well for lodges' autonomy, for it allows those with more of a cultural or religious background to stay away from the ones that aren't similarly minded. So a lodge in a European part of town wouldn't come into conflict with one in an American neighborhood that might have some different rituals and rites.

This takes us to what the Freemasons call "regularity," or how Grand Lodges give each other mutual recognition. This allows members in any lodge to visit and attend meetings in another Grand Lodge's jurisdiction if they're recognized, and vice versa. It's simply a way for a Freemason to visit another part of the world and partake of the brotherhood's rituals in a new setting. Lodges that mutually recognize each other are said to be *in amity.* Now Grand Lodges like the UGLE and GOdF that are *not* in amity don't allow formal interaction with each other or their jurisdictions; nevertheless, informal visitation can usually still be arranged, albeit with certain restrictions.

The individual lodge is still the basic building block of Freemasonry. When members meet, they meet *as* a lodge—it's a misnomer to say that they're meeting *in* a lodge. Although they may indeed be meeting in a structure that they call a "lodge," "temple" (of art and philosophy), "hall," or "center," the members are considered the lodge, not the building they're meeting in. Early lodges met in taverns and public places, and it's not unusual for those in the present day to share the same building.

Requirements to become a member of Freemasonry aren't that stringent, with a potential candidate just needing to apply to his local lodge by asking an existing member for introduction. (Depending on the jurisdiction, a lodge may require one or two references from current Masons.) In order to become a Freemason, you must be elected to be a candidate by the lodge in secret ballot and must meet these general requirements:

1. Be a man who comes of his own free will.

2. Believe in a supreme being (or in a few jurisdictions, a creative principle).

3. Be at least the minimum age (18 to 25, but most commonly 21).

4. Be of sound mind, body, and good morals,

and of good repute.
5. Be free.

6. Have one or two references from current Masons (depending on jurisdiction).

Other than minor variations from the above (for instance the requirement to "be free" is strictly a historical rule and has been eliminated in many lodges), that's all that's needed to become a Mason. There are, of course, dues to pay (which tend to be very reasonable), but then you're initiated into the lodge in its first degree.

Regular Freemasonry—also known as "Craft" or "Blue Lodge Freemasonry"—has three degrees or levels:

1. *Entered Apprentice (EA)—First Degree*
2. *Fellow Craft (FC)—Second Degree*
3. *Master Mason (MM)—Third Degree*

Each degree requires learning certain subject matter before going on to the next one, just as in the building trades with the positions of apprentice, journeyman, and master craftsman. In some jurisdictions, a man is a Freemason when he first becomes an Entered Apprentice; while in others he must be a Master Mason in order to be recognized in the order. Regardless, all Blue Lodge or Craft Freemasonry considers the degree of Master Mason to be the highest. Thus, a first-degree Mason would be an Entered Apprentice, while a third-degree member would be a Master Mason.

Besides regular (Craft or Blue Lodge) Freemasonry, there are several other offshoots that are significant— these are the Scottish Rite of Freemasonry; the York Rite of Freemasonry; and the Shrine (or "Shriners," as they're more commonly known), whose full name is "Ancient Arabic Order of the Nobles of the Mystic Shrine." Both the Scottish and York Rites exist throughout the world, while the Shrine is only in North America, with its focus on the United States. The Shrine is known for its children's hospitals and burn institutes where treatment is free, and is perhaps the most public of all Freemasonry organizations thanks to this charitable work.

The Scottish and York Rites came out of the desire of some Masons to further contemplate what's taught in the Craft or Blue Lodges, perhaps including more lessons on the esoteric studies they'd already learned in becoming a Master Mason. In the Scottish Rite, they give numbers in addition to the third-degree Master Mason (from 4 to 33, with the 33rd degree being honorary) to recognize these further studies. It must be made clear here, however, that a 33rd-degree Master Mason is no more a "master" than one of the 3rd degree. To emphasize this point, in Europe it may take months or even years to obtain each degree, while in the United States they're often conferred during special weekend "convocations."

Additional degrees were also added in the York Rite, but they weren't numbered. The highest degree in this order is that of Knight Templar, but here again, any Master Mason has just as much power as a Knight Templar Master Mason. Freemasonry tends to look at all of this very simply: A Master Mason is a Master Mason, just as a high school graduate is a high school graduate, regardless of whether or not he or she took special classes.

In addition to the Craft, Scottish Rite, York Rite, and Shrine orders, there are several other organizations that are related to Freemasonry. These groups give the opportunity to women—and teenagers and children of both sexes—to participate in associations that have similar ideals to those of Freemasonry. These include Grotto, Tall Cedars of Lebanon, Order of the Eastern Star, Job's Daughters, International Order of the Rainbow for Girls, Order of DeMolay, National Sojourners, High Twelve, Daughters of the Nile, the Mystic Order of Veiled Prophets of the Enchanted Realm, and the Knights of the Red Cross of Constantine, among many others.

Rituals and Faith

Freemasons use signs (hand gestures), grips (handshakes), and passwords to gain admission to their meetings and to identify whether a visitor is legitimate. The bulk of the evidence I found pointed out that this practice didn't start until the mid-1600s, when nonoperative members had been admitted to lodges. Many claimed to have revealed these communication devices (and probably did), but local jurisdictions create their *own* rituals and change them fairly frequently.

The motto of the Freemasons could very well be "Liberty, equality, fraternity" (several conspiracy theorists have even put forth that they helped instigate the French Revolution), but their actual creed goes something like this: "Morality in which all men agree; that is, to be good men and true."

Many people have said that the order is actually a religion (which members emphatically deny), and it does indeed have what we might call religious overtones. Joseph Fort Newton, a noted authority in the Masonic world and an Episcopal minister, once said that "Masonry is not a religion, but Religion; not a church but a worship in which men of all religions may unite."

Although Freemasonry isn't a religion or church, it does seem to be more of a worship in which men of all faiths may unite for fellowship and good. Yet many in the hierarchy of the Vatican consider it to be a secret society that's plotting against Catholics and trying to bring about a single worldwide belief system. Well, if brotherhood is to be considered something sinister, then we're all in trouble.

Francine says that the views of Freemasonry that promote religious tolerance also come into direct conflict with so-called Bible Christianity. "Biblical Christians" (or what we might term the conservative branch of Protestant Christianity, which would include evangelicals) have always been adamant that a person can only be saved by Jesus Christ. I find this to be in direct opposition to what Christianity truly is, especially when many Biblical Christians don't think of Freemasons as Christian.

This is especially ironic when you consider that some church denominations have a great many leaders who are avowed Masons. For example, the Southern Baptist Convention (SBC) Sunday School Board found in a 1991 survey that 14 percent of SBC pastors and 18 percent of SBC deacons were Masons, and it's estimated that more than 33 percent of total U.S. lodge membership is filled by SBC members. In 2000, a report put out by the SBC said that more than 1,000 of its pastors are Masons. Is Freemasonry now the secret tool of the Southern Baptists to take over American religion? Of course not . . . but I wouldn't put it past a conspiracy theorist to postulate some kind of scheme regarding this.

Freemasons do refer to the Bible as a volume of sacred law, but only in a so-called Christian lodge. In other words, Hebrew scrolls are used in a Hebrew lodge, the Koran in a Muslim lodge, the Vedas in a Brahmin lodge, and so forth. The Hebrew Kabbalah's teachings can also be seen in many of the mystical and philosophical degrees of Masonry; for example, their ritual of a "search for light" leads directly back to the Kabbalah.

In fact, rituals in Freemasonry can often be traced back to Hinduism, Buddhism, Zoroastrianism, Islam, and other Eastern religions, as well as Christianity and Judaism. Again, I feel that this is their attempt to put every faith under the same umbrella with perfect acceptance. Although the order puts forth the belief in a supreme being or creative power, individual members aren't required to say which god they believe in. Many Masons say that the G in their great Geometer stands for "God," but they also believe that the true name of God has been lost.

Freemasonry omits the mention of Jesus due to the risk of offending those who aren't Christian. They believe that Christians are a sect because they only accept Jesus Christ as Lord, to the exclusion of all others—and many lodges also believe that there were *many* messiahs.

Sin isn't mentioned by Masons because they believe that human shortcomings can be overcome by greater spirituality and enlightenment through learning. In fact, as members get older, they're encouraged to happily reflect on a well-spent life of learning. Because they don't believe in sin, they don't believe in "salvation" in the biblical sense, which rules out hell and the awful book of Revelation. In the end, it gets down to the fact that Masons don't change their beliefs to fit the Bible; the Bible is adjusted to fit their beliefs.

The taking of oaths is obligatory as one progresses on to become a Master Mason, as is the initiation oath, which is mandatory in order to become accepted as a candidate for Freemasonry. The following oath may deviate somewhat, depending on the lodge location:

> I most solemnly and sincerely promise and swear that I will always hail, ever conceal, and never reveal, any of the arts, parts, or points of the hidden mysteries of ancient Freemasonry.
>
> All this I most solemnly, sincerely promise and swear, with a firm and steadfast resolution to perform the same, without any mental reservation or secret evasion of mine whatever binding myself under no less a penalty than that of having my throat cut across, my tongue torn out by its roots, and buried in the rough sand of the sea at low-water mark where the tide ebbs and flows twice in 24 hours, should I ever knowingly or willingly violate my solemn oath and obligation as an Entered Apprentice Mason. So help me, God.

Masons and the Birth of a Nation

The main reason why I wanted to include Free-ma-sonry in this book's section on political secret societies is because of the way they've affected the founding of the United States of America. You see, Francine says that the order took hold in the U.S. as a rebuttal to the religious suppression in England and the Inquisitions of the Catholic Church, which were the main reasons why they became a secret society. It was done for protection.

The first American lodges appeared in Philadelphia in 1730 and Boston in 1733, and most of the country's founding fathers were Freemasons—including George Washington, Benjamin Franklin, Ethan Allen, John Hancock, John Paul Jones, Paul Revere, and some 35 others who either signed the Declaration of Independence or the Constitution. (Conversely, the following early Americans condemned the organization: John Adams, John Quincy Adams, James Madison, Millard Fillmore, Daniel Webster, and Charles Sumner.)

There's no doubt that the order played a fairly large part in the founding of the United States. For example, there are words in the Constitution and Declaration of Independence that smack of its influence, and we see their symbolism on the dollar bill—the uncompleted pyramid with the all-seeing eye, the number of feathers on the eagle's spread wings, and the stars above the eagle's head in the shape of the Star of David all seem to come from it. And the mottos of *e pluribus unum* ("out of many, one") and *novus ordo seclorum* ("a new order of the ages") give hints to the New World Order that Free-masonry appears to desire.

At least 13 U.S. Presidents have been Masons; numerous movie stars such as Gene Autry, Ernest Borgnine,

Eddie Cantor, Douglas Fairbanks, W. C. Fields, Glenn Ford, Clark Gable, Oliver Hardy, Al Jolson, Tom Mix, Audie Murphy, Roy Rogers, Will Rogers, Peter Sellers, Danny Thomas, and John Wayne; entertainment moguls and talents like Count Basie, Mel Blanc, Nat King Cole, Cecil B. DeMille, Duke Ellington, D. W. Griffith, Arthur Godfrey, Harry Houdini, Louis B. Mayer, John Phillip Sousa, Lowell Thomas, Jack Warner, William Wyler, Darryl F. Zanuck, and Florenz Ziegfeld; famous explorers and astronauts including Admiral Richard E. Byrd, Kit Carson, "Buffalo Bill" Cody, Virgil "Gus" Grissom, Charles Lindbergh, Edgar D. Mitchell, Admiral Robert E. Peary, Wally Schirra, and both Meriwether Lewis and William Clark; sports stars such as Cy Young, Honus Wagner, Arnold Palmer, Rogers Hornsby, Curt Gowdy, and Ty Cobb; politicians and leaders including General Omar N. Bradley, William Jennings Bryan, Winston Churchill, Robert J. Dole, General James Doolittle, William O. Douglas, Barry Goldwater, J. Edgar Hoover, Sam Houston, Reverend Jesse Jackson, Fiorello LaGuardia, General Douglas MacArthur, Norman Vincent Peale, Joseph Smith, Strom Thurmond, Earl Warren, and Brigham Young; writers and composers like Irving Berlin, Robert Burns, Samuel Clemens (Mark Twain), George M. Cohan, Sir Arthur Conan Doyle, Rudyard Kipling, Wolfgang Amadeus Mozart, Sir Walter Scott, and Jonathan Swift; and moguls and businessmen such as John Jacob Astor, Walter Chrysler, Samuel Colt, Henry Ford, Rowland Hussey Macy, Andrew Mellon, and James C. Penney. And this is only scratching the surface of the list of famous Masons!

While many opponents of Freemasonry feel that its members are being deceived and hoodwinked, taking a look at the list of famous people above tells me that there would have been an awfully large number of intelligent and crafty people being fooled, which is highly unlikely. We can also see that Masons come from all walks of life; conversely, most secret societies that have specific agendas tend to be overloaded with a certain type of person with similar thoughts and ideas. It's awfully hard to imagine sports stars, astronauts, and businesspeople all getting together in order to overthrow the world.

The interesting part about Freemasonry is that it tries to incorporate so much esoteric information from so many repositories of knowledge. It's almost as if its founders had to try to integrate every possible school of thought in order to be as diverse as possible in dealing with their philosophies and beliefs. If you look back at the origins of different cultures, you'll undoubtedly find some myth or legend that the Masons refer to as being part of their beginnings. From Adam and Eve to ancient giant aliens or avatars in the Sumerian civilization; from the building of the Temple of Solomon with Hiram Abif to the ancient Egyptians like Hatshepsut or Akhenaton; from the Essenes and Gnostics to King Arthur, the School of Alexandria, the Knights Templar, Plato, Jesus and his apostles, Mohammed, Hermes, Hebrews, the Schools of India and Persia; and on and on it goes. Freemasons supposedly have their finger in every ancient mystery that's ever existed on this earth. In doing so, they evidently felt that they had all the bases covered and could truly be a fraternity of men able to embrace anyone from any culture or religion in brotherhood.

Freemasonry survived because its members were builders who were needed to erect great churches and temples to God. Perhaps that's why they escaped perse-cution—after all, who would suspect dusty stonemasons, whose talent was to build the great edifices that human-kind felt it needed? Then, just like the early Christians, they met covertly to advance their knowledge and their own agendas, which led to their getting into politics, economy, and law.

There's no doubt that Freemasonry is one of the old-est (and, at various times, most powerful) secret societies that the world has known. Whether its beginnings were thousands of years ago or, as Francine says, about 1,700 years ago, it really doesn't matter. The order still exists and continues to have quite an impact. Its charitable works have helped humankind, and there are thousands of good people who call themselves Freemasons who are out there helping others in our world today.

Conspiracy theorists want to believe that Freemasonry is running America and the world, but I can find no con-clusive evidence that this is taking place. While Francine claims that the Masons, as a society, are for a New World Order, many who work for it don't have the power or the political clout they once did. I personally feel that none of us need worry about the Masons—yes, they may have some hidden agendas under their cultivated exterior, but they're not a global threat in any way.

PART II

RELIGIOUS SOCIETIES

CHAPTER 6

THE KNIGHTS TEMPLAR

*M*y dear friend Gordon Smith, an excellent psychic and medium from Scotland, related an interesting story to me one evening. After I mentioned that I was writing a book on secret societies, he started talking about one of his visits to the Theosophical Society in London (a place I've been three times myself).

It seems that Gordon was killing some time before a lecture when he happened upon the graveyard of a small church near the society's headquarters. He noticed three crumbling headstones dating from the 13th century that had no names, merely the symbol of a skull and crossbones upon them. Most of the other graves were more recent and in better condition, so Gordon asked the priest at the church about the old ones he'd seen. Although the priest seemed very reluctant to answer, my friend persisted and inquired whether or not they were Knights Templar graves, as the skull and crossbones was one of their symbols. The priest immediately said that Gordon was mistaken and that he'd appreciate it if my friend would never visit that graveyard again. My psychic pal shrugged it off and proceeded to go to the Theosophical Society to give his talk.

When Gordon had spoken at this location once before, he'd noticed a large symbol of the Freemasons along one wall. When he asked some people attending the lecture about it, they told him that at one time a symbol of the Rosy Cross (an emblem of the Rosicrucian Order) had also been present. When he questioned members of the Theosophical Society about the images, they declared that the information he'd been given was incorrect . . . as was what he'd seen with his own eyes. Gordon said that he left somewhat puzzled, and concluded his story by asking me why all of the symbols he'd seen were denied by both the church and the Theosophical Society.

I answered him in the same way in which I'll begin getting into the substance of this chapter: There's *so* much controversy surrounding covert organizations, especially where the Knights Templar are concerned. Historians have one take on the origins of this group, while theologians have another slant, and believers in the Holy Grail present it in still another light. So after mounds (and I mean literally *mounds*) of research, I believe that I've managed to come up with the truth as to what these folks were all about.

The Knights Templar are probably one of the most fascinating and mysterious secret societies of all—not only because of their hidden and seemingly bizarre actions, but also because they seem so contradictory in nature. For example, they were brutal in warfare, giving no mercy and expecting none, but they were also seen as highly religious and pious. And while they became rather astute in matters of finance and accumulated great wealth, the Templars felt that their greatest treasure could never be measured in worldly goods.

What Is a Knight?

Before we delve further into the Knights Templar, let's explore where the concept of knights in general came from. For all intents and purposes, knighthood and chivalry are synonymous with each other: The term *knighthood* comes from the English word *knight* (from the Old English word *cniht,* which means "boy," or "servant"); while *chivalry* stems from the French word *chevalerie,* which itself comes from *chevalier* or "knight." In addition, the German translation for *knight* is *ritter* (literally, "rider").

The simplest way to define knights is "professional soldiers," and they started to become prominent as early as the 10th century, toward the end of the feudal era. In the early days, there was no real class distinction between them and the general population, as just about anyone who had the wherewithal (and money) to obtain the training and equipment could follow their path. However, as knighthood emerged into the 11th century, it turned into a primarily professional association, with its members being small landholders, builders, free men, and the like.

In the 12th century, a religious aspect was added to knighthood, with many monks becoming true *miles Christi* ("soldiers of Christ"). This religious influence also brought with it a code of ethics and behavior that became what we now call "chivalry." In the latter portion of the century, literature lent a hand by romanticizing and glorifying knighthood. And although these men weren't necessarily nobles, and members of the aristocracy weren't all knights, the two did begin to merge about this time.

As the 13th century dawned, knights were almost exclusively the sons of existing knights or nobles, and for the most part no longer soldiers. You see, thanks to the increasing use of mercenaries and the development of gunpowder and more powerful archery, knights became less effective in actual combat. Yet the ideas of chivalry continued to live on, and over the next two centuries knights became more like entertainers as they participated in tournaments to demonstrate their skills. This period was also the start of heraldry, where one noble house was distinguished from another by making its own coat of arms.

During the Crusades, groups of knights would band together to protect or help pilgrims, as well as fight for the Holy Land. After their military might was no longer needed, these "orders of knighthood" evolved into the awards and decorations of modern times. Only a few of the ancient orders survive to this day, such as the Knights of Malta (which I shall discuss in the next chapter). However, in my research I found no fewer than 200 different orders or classes proclaiming to be knights—while many countries still have them, they're more like fraternal organizations. In some cases, they also distinguish the classes of nobility and are strictly honorary in nature.

Most people equate knighthood with the romanticized accounts of King Arthur, the search for the Holy Grail (which is believed to be the cup Jesus drank from at the Last Supper and in which his blood was caught when he was on the cross), or fictional heroes such as Ivanhoe. In reality, knights reached their zenith at the time of the Crusades, as they tried to win the Holy Land from the Muslims and went on their quests to find relics of Christendom, including the Grail.

However, scholars, historians, and theologians don't believe that knights fought for the Holy Land or went in search of relics just because of their religious zeal. The plain fact is that many of these supposedly chivalrous gentlemen raped, pillaged, and plundered anything they could get their hands on. Life at that time was extremely harsh, and those in service to protect or serve some higher purpose could also be brutal in their treatment of other human beings.

While early knights helped guard caravan and trade routes and escorted travelers and pilgrims, many had agreements with liege lords to protect their property from petty disputes. They were also often called to arms if a king needed troops to fight a war. And after the first Crusade was initiated by Pope Urban II in 1095, the Knights Templar formed. Their story is not only mysterious and fascinating, but supposedly heretical as well.

The Birth of the Knights Templar

The Knights Templar were definitely members of a secret society, although they didn't start out that way; in fact, historians and scholars tend to agree that their motives were downright pious at the beginning. While very few records of the group have survived, most experts say that they first banded together in the year 1118. (Some believe that it was actually earlier, in 1099 or 1111.)

The order's founders are believed to have been a French nobleman named Hughes de Payens, who became the first Grand Master of the Templars, and Flemish knight Godfrey de Saint-Omer. These two were the ones who went before Baldwin II (Jerusalem's king at the time) to ask that "the Poor Knights of Christ and of the Temple of Solomon" (also called "Brethren of the Soldiery of the Temple")—which would then simply be called "the Knights Templar"—be recognized. And it's said that the order's seal (two knights riding on one horse, indicating poverty) is taken from the fact that Hughes and Godfrey had only one horse between them, which they shared.

Most of those who believe that 1118 was the Templars' founding date rely on *A History of Deeds Done Beyond the Sea,* which was written by the Archbishop of Acre, William of Tyre (1130–1185). Yet this volume isn't considered that reliable by modern experts, as several errors have been found. For example, although the book gives 1118 as the founding date of the Knights Templar, claiming that it was started by nine knights who didn't allow new members to join for at least nine years, other records indicate that the Count of Anjou was the first new member, and the date given for his acceptance was 1120. If you subtract nine years from 1120, you get the year 1111.

My guide Francine says that the Order of the Knights Templar was actually founded about 1099 under a different name by a man known as Godefroy de Bouillon

(Godfrey of Bouillon), one of the leaders of the first Crusade. According to Francine, Godfrey was a fairly pious man who immediately responded to the call of Pope Urban II to free the Holy Land from the Muslims. He set off in 1096 to lead an army of approximately 40,000 men from Lorraine, France, finally arriving in Jerusalem in early 1099. Godfrey then proceeded to lay siege to the city, participating in the slaughter of almost every Muslim and Jew who resided there. In *The Monks of War,* Desmond Seward describes this massacre as follows:

> Jerusalem was stormed in July 1099. The rabid ferocity of its sack showed just how little the [Catholic] Church had succeeded in Christianizing atavistic instincts. The entire population of the Holy City was put to the sword, Jews as well as Muslims, 70,000 men, women, and children perished in a holocaust which raged for three days. In places men waded in blood up to their ankles and horsemen were splashed by it as they rode through the streets. Weeping, these devout conquerors went barefoot to pray at the Holy Sepulchre before rushing eagerly back to the slaughter.

As an aside, at this time the Catholic Church did not deem it a sin to kill those whom they considered to be "infidels" in possession of the Holy Land. In fact, they considered the execution of these people to be a way that Christians could atone for their sins, thereby gaining them admittance to heaven. In contrast, after Muslims conquered a city, they'd offer amnesty and safe departure to survivors— even to soldiers who had fought against them.

It certainly appears that the Muslims were much more "Christian" than so-called Christians were at that time. Saladin, the great Muslim sultan and warrior, was especially merciful in taking back the Holy Land and Jerusalem from the Christian crusaders, and was even widely respected by Christian soldiers as being chivalrous. It's also known that even though England's King Richard I (known as "Richard the Lionheart") and Saladin never met in battle, Saladin offered Richard his physicians when the king was wounded; in another battle, when Richard lost his horse, Saladin sent him three steeds to replace it. This man was also the one who helped negotiate a treaty in which the Holy Land would remain under Muslim control, but Christian pilgrimage would be allowed in safety.

Getting back to Godfrey of Bouillon . . . after he captured Jerusalem in 1099, he was made king of that city, which he promptly refused. Instead, he accepted the title of "Protector of the Holy Sepulchre." Francine says that on the way to Jerusalem, Godfrey became enamored with the beliefs and teachings of a group of Calabrian monks who'd established the Order of Sion (which I'll cover in Chapter 9)—to the point that they confided in him some of their secret knowledge about the survival, marriage, and children of Jesus Christ (all of which I'll explain in detail in Chapter 14). This was especially interesting to Godfrey because his ancestors were the Merovingian kings, which Christ's lineage was supposedly traced to. (I personally find it interesting that the Calabrian monks originally came from the area of Calabria in Italy, which was known to be the home of the Pythagorean school and was also the origin of the "heresies" of the monk Joachim of Fiore . . . so that area was very Gnostic.)

Knowing that Godfrey was one of the major leaders of the Crusades, this group of monks formed a sort of alliance with him that would work for them both if and when Jerusalem was conquered. Francine explains that after Godfrey took the office of Protector of the Holy Sepulchre, he formed the Order of the Holy Sepulchre, a group of 12 knights who were devoted to protecting the religious chapter of canons that had been serving at the Sepulchre of Christ before Jerusalem had even been conquered by the crusaders. These knights would eventually evolve into the Knights Templar soon after Godfrey's death in July 1100.

Godfrey's passing was unexpected and remains a mystery. Some say that he was pierced by an arrow while besieging the city of Acre, while others believe that he was poisoned by the Emir of Caesarea. Nevertheless, his death left a temporary vacuum of leadership in the newly formed Order of the Holy Sepulchre, which was soon filled by French nobleman Hughes de Payens. There was also the still-unresolved issue of who would be king of Jerusalem, as several men vied for the noble office. Ultimately, Godfrey's brother was crowned King Baldwin I of Jerusalem. After his death eight years later, his cousin Baldwin II took the throne.

Following the well-laid-out plan left by Godfrey, the Order obtained the aid of the monks from Calabria and managed to persuade King Baldwin II to recognize a new group of knights, which they called the "Order of the Poor Knights of Christ and the Temple of Solomon" (better known as the Knights Templar). Ostensibly, this new organization would protect pilgrims traveling to the Holy Land. The Order also persuaded Baldwin to allow the monks of Calabria to form a new religious brotherhood and to provide both the Templars and the friars with a place for their headquarters and abbey.

Baldwin gave them a prime spot in Jerusalem: the Temple Mount, which was the site of the Jewish Temple built by Solomon. The Calabrian monks formed the Order of Sion and constructed an abbey named "Notre Dame du Mont Sion"; and the Knights Templar built their headquarters in the spot that used to be the stables of King Solomon, adjoining the royal palace on the Temple Mount (today Al-Aqsa Mosque).

Francine states that in addition to Godfrey, two other knights in the original Order of the Holy Sepulchre died, which left the Templars with only nine members. Although they were supposed to be protectors of pilgrims to the Holy Land, Francine says that they instead dedicated themselves to another project for almost ten years, one that developed out of the knowledge that they'd received from the monks of the Order of Sion.

The Templars' Treasure

One of the greatest mysteries about the Knights Templar was how they started out as an order dedicated to poverty but suddenly became one of the wealthiest and most powerful organizations in the world almost overnight. Well, Francine explains that the Templars started digging beneath the old Temple of Solomon site on the Temple Mount in the hopes of finding religious artifacts, particularly the Ark of the Covenant (in which the Ten Commandments are said to lie). That's because the Order of Sion, based on the knowledge that they'd acquired over the centuries, had told them that the Temple was the most likely place to find the Ark.

Francine claims that after nine years of digging, the Templars found an artifact that has never been mentioned in any historical book that I know of: a type of journal enclosed in a gold box that was like a miniature copy of the Ark of the Covenant. The solid gold box was a treasure in itself, but the writings inside were even more valuable. They were somewhat autobiographical in nature, describing events, times, and places that the writer had experienced . . . a writer who was none other than Jesus Christ.

This journal outlined all the Lord's travels in India, Persia, and Egypt before his public ministry began, as well as many of the teachings he'd learned and then disseminated to his disciples. It also described his associations with the Essenes and Ebonites (of which Christ's brother, James, was purportedly a leader) and outlined the most startling information of all—that he survived the Crucifixion and escaped to France!

According to Francine, this is where the journal ended. She also says that it was Joseph of Arimathea who buried the gold casket with the journal at the request of Jesus after he'd been in France for several years, for he knew that it would be discovered someday. It seems that Joseph of Arimathea was more of a hero than anyone has ever known. As you'll see in Chapter 14, he not only played a role in saving Jesus from death, but also helped the great teacher escape and settle in France. He then established Christianity in Britain and also assisted in burying this "history of Christ" under the Temple Mount.

Many scholars and historians believe that what the Knights Templar found were the lost riches of the Jewish Temple, which would account for the order's sudden upsurge of wealth. The "Templar treasure" has always been legendary in nature, with continual speculation about what it consisted of. Francine says that while the treasure wasn't of monetary value, it did bring these men great wealth and power.

My spirit guide points out that at first the Knights Templar didn't know what to do with their fantastic find, so they consulted monks in the Order of Sion (who, after all, had given them the idea to dig in the first place). After some debate, they decided to notify the Catholic Church of their discovery. But since they really didn't trust the Church, they took some steps to ensure that their find would remain safely hidden. They made several copies of the original writings and sent one of them directly to the pope; at the same time, they placed the original writings in a secret location for safekeeping.

When the pope got his copy, he became upset and made arrangements to see the original writings by sending his own designated experts back to Jerusalem. Upon arrival, the scholars were blindfolded and taken to the secret location of the original journal. They were then allowed—under supervision—to view and study the writings for authenticity. Since science was very archaic at that time (early 12th century), verification would have to have been made via the language used and comparisons with other known writings. Obviously, there was no carbon dating and scientific analysis at their disposal as there is today.

Suffice it to say that several years after the pope's experts returned to Rome, the Knights Templar began accumulating great wealth. It started with the Order being recognized and championed by St. Bernard of Clairvaux, one of the most powerful and influential monks at that time. Due to his influence, the "Rule of the Knights by Papal Bull to the Order" gave them legal autonomy to the point where they only had to answer to the pope and

God Himself. The pope gave his official approval of the group in 1139; and from that time on, the knights were granted land, castles, and economic support from kings and other nobility throughout all of Christian Europe.

Now was this blackmail on the part of the Knights Templar or just a prudent stand taken by the Catholic Church? Francine says it was a little of both. The Church certainly had knowledge about various Gnostic and heretical beliefs at the time, as evinced by a letter written by a famous monk named Gerbert of Aurillac (who later became Pope Sylvester II) some 100 years before the first Crusade. The future pontiff said something to the effect that he hoped France would recover the holy places so that a search could be made for the keys to the "Universal Understanding" hidden there. This shows that the Church was aware that there were religious artifacts hidden in the Holy Land, and that many of the Gnostic and heretical sects claimed to know right where they were.

As I mentioned earlier, Godfrey of Bouillon came by a great deal of information from Calabrian monks who eventually became the Priory of Sion. This knowledge was most certainly passed on to the Templars; and in their digging, they came across some articles that bore this knowledge.

It's also interesting that the Knights Templar constructed several other structures in various holy places. The abbey that they built for the Order of Sion was just by the Zion Gate in Jerusalem; and they made additions or renovations to other sites that included the Tomb of David, the Cenacle, and the ancient Church of the Apostles. Francine states that the Templars added to the building of the Church of the Apostles by constructing the Chapel of the Holy Spirit, and they tacked on a room called "the Chamber of Mysteries" (perhaps relating to the ancient knowledge that they now possessed).

The Knights Templar were becoming more and more secretive and mysterious in nature. Could this be because of the scrolls and artifacts that they'd discovered in Jerusalem? Well, recent archaeological digs have unearthed evidence of a community of Essenes who also lived on Mount Zion at one time. (Before this discovery, the Essenes were thought only to have resided at Qumran, near the Dead Sea.)

The Templars were also renowned for their knowledge in construction, ultimately building hundreds of churches, many in either a round or octagonal shape that was supposedly copied from the design of the Holy Sepulchre in Jerusalem. This would seem to back up Francine's assertion that the Knights had learned some of the ancient mysteries from the Order of Sion or from their recovered holy artifacts, for the ancient hermetic mysteries contained much about geometry and building practices.

Perhaps one of the biggest misconceptions about the wealth of the Knights Templar comes from those who think that they got the bulk of it from blackmailing the Church. The truth is that the Templars' riches primarily came from their skills in what were essentially the beginnings of banking. You see, the Templars established a system in which a person could deposit money at any one of a number of Templar houses and receive a coded receipt that could be produced at another house to receive their money. This allowed travelers, pilgrims, and merchants to take journeys without the danger of having money on their person stolen; and it revolutionized the transfer of funds from one part of the land to another.

Of course, the Templars received a fee for this service. They also loaned money out to nobles and kings, receiving interest in return. As they were known to be the first medieval bankers in Europe, most of their wealth came from this business. They also accumulated land and castles from many who entered the society, as well as from nobles who defaulted on loans or just donated a portion of their holdings to the Order. At their peak of power, the Templars owned at least 870 castles and preceptories (subsidiary houses), with accompanying lands or estates throughout Christendom.

In addition, they had a considerable number of ships, which constituted a great navy that could carry goods or help protect their vast estates and properties. Interestingly enough, one of the Templar symbols—the skull and crossbones—was flown as a flag on their ships. Was this symbol adopted by pirates because of the downfall of the Templars as supposed heretics? Or did former members turn to piracy after the group was dissolved by Pope Clement V, and successive buccaneers just adopted the symbol? Francine says it was the latter.

The Decline of the Order

The Knights Templar were very active in the Holy Land for many years, and their relationship with the Priory of Sion seems to have been one of mutual leadership until they had a parting of the ways in 1188. The dissolution of the partnership of these two orders might have been directly related to the fall of Jerusalem to Saladin in 1187—the Order of Sion was allowed to remain in their abbey in that city, while the Knights Templar were forced to retreat and fight numerous battles elsewhere. The Templars did manage to help take back Acre in 1191, which was where they resided until 1291. Saladin had enacted numerous truces to allow Christian pilgrimage, but constant attacks from Christian armies eventually tried the patience of the Muslims, who managed to effectively drive away all such armies from the Holy Land by 1291.

Although nine major Crusades and numerous smaller ones were instigated during these times (mostly by the Catholic Church but also by various rulers), they were largely ineffective and usually resulted in disaster. Only the first Crusade and the one against the Cathars (which I'll cover later on) were what we might term successful.

After their defeat at Acre, the surviving Templars escaped from the Holy Land on their ships to join their brethren in Europe, who'd been accumulating great riches from their banking practices. Unfortunately, this wealth eventually played a large part in their downfall. As the Templars loaned out more and more money, many nobles went deeper into debt . . . and even worse, became extremely envious. One of these was France's monarch, Philippe le Bel, or "Philip the Fair," who got his name from his looks—not from his dealings with others. By 1306, King Philip was deeply in debt to the Knights Templar due to his lavish lifestyle and the increasing costs of warfare, and he tried to alleviate his financial constraints by confiscating all Jewish lands and wealth. Then he taxed all Catholic churches in his realm, to the tune of half their earnings, which brought him no end of conflict.

Pope Boniface VIII issued a papal bull that essentially said that Church lands and assets couldn't be taxed by any monarch, and Philip had him arrested. Although he was released after three days, Boniface passed away shortly thereafter.

After the death of Boniface VIII in October 1303, it took more than a year to elect the next pontiff due to schisms in the Church. Aided by King Philip (who definitely wanted a French pope), Clement V was finally elected in November 1304. Considered by most historians to have been a weak leader who was basically "in the pocket" of King Philip, Clement V is known for two things in his reign:

1. The moving of the Roman Curia to Avignon, France, in 1309

2. His aid in the suppression of the Knights Templar (the effort begun by Philip the Fair)

Since Philip was heavily in debt to the Templars and desirous of their wealth, he'd tried to enter their order in 1306 but was roundly and decisively refused entry. Infuriated beyond belief, King Philip ordered the arrest of the Templars on charges of heresy on Friday, October 13, 1307. (Some believe that the superstition of Friday the 13th being unlucky originated from this action.) Jacques de Molay, the Grand Master of the Knights Templar at the time, and 60 others were captured and imprisoned in Paris, along with another 15,000 members in other areas in France. The charges levied against them included intercourse with demons, worshipping familiars, sodomy, and black magic.

For the next several years, the captured Templars were tortured unmercifully with hot irons and other infamous instruments of torment. In fact, Jacques de Molay is said to have had his hands and feet nailed to a door. With all of the agony being inflicted, many of the Templars died—but several also confessed to various charges of heresy, ranging from sodomy (which three supposedly admitted) to worshipping a head they called "Baphomet," having intercourse with demons, and spitting on the cross (which some owned up to). Most scholars consider these confessions to simply be untrue because they were obtained under duress.

However, some experts interestingly point out that the confessions of spitting on the cross may have indeed been factual because of the Templars' involvement with the early "Jewish Christians." They theorize that because these Jewish Christians didn't believe in the Divinity of Jesus and instead put forth that he was only a man, part of the initiation into the Order of Knights Templar included spitting on the cross to disavow the Trinity and the Divinity of Christ. This could very well have been the case, especially when you consider that what the society found under the Temple Mount proved that Christ had survived the Crucifixion.

Francine confirms that the Templars' view on Jesus was very much like the Jewish Christian belief—that he was a man and not Divine, but that his teachings *were* inspired by God. While the Knights Templar did strongly believe in God, they didn't accept Jesus as a part of the Holy Trinity or as a "son of God."

The few Templars who didn't confess, or who recanted their confessions because they were induced under torment, were convicted of heresy and burned at the stake. In the case of Jacques de Molay, after being tortured for almost seven years, he finally gave up in 1314. Although he recanted his confession, Philip had the man burned at the stake on the Île de la Cité (near the cathedral of Notre Dame). As Jacques de Molay died, he supposedly cried out that King Philip and Pope Clement would be called for judgment before God very soon for their actions (and both men did die within the year).

Public pressure regarding the Knights Templar caused Philip the Fair to turn over their fate to Pope Clement V. Although the pontiff was essentially under the king's control, he was also sympathetic to the Templars because they weren't persecuted outside of France—in fact, they'd been found innocent of all charges in trials in other countries such as Germany, Portugal, and Spain. Pope Clement devised a compromise in 1312 when he dissolved the Order of the Knights Templar and gave all their assets to the Knights Hospitaller of St. John (also known as the Knights of Malta), and kept their punishment in his own merciful hands.

The Knights Templar were now finished, and their time of "Camelot," much like King Arthur himself, faded into history. The Catholic Church got the bulk of their wealth and many of the relics they'd concealed, which are now safely hidden away. It seems almost too coincidental that every time some individual or group came close to finding out the truth about Jesus in those days, they were branded as heretics and killed.

The End . . . or Is It?

While the Knights Templar supposedly ended, some of the surviving members joined the Knights Hospitaller, while others formed orders with different names, such as the Knights of Christ in Portugal and the Knights of Montessa in Spain. Some Templars are even said to have traveled to the New World, more than 100 years before Columbus. While scholars tend to reject this latter claim, new archaeological discoveries in Nova Scotia that are now being studied might bear out this story.

The tragedy of the Knights Templar is that they grew too powerful and wealthy. From their formation with nine pious knights spurred by the fanaticism of the first Crusade, to their fall with thousands being imprisoned and tortured, the times dictated their fate. Keep in mind that the medieval era wasn't easy, what with religious zeal and fanaticism running rampant, along with the constant vying for position, power, and wealth by myriad kings and other rulers. It was bound to create an environment where cruelty and warfare were in abundance and the poor just tried to survive. It was also an age when the middle class didn't exist, for the rich abused the poor into virtual slavery. Nobles and kings were constantly trying to obtain land, wealth, and power, using the lower class as fodder for their wars and to bring in their crops.

The Knights Templar were certainly a part of these times and were no saints themselves—they were fierce and cruel in their dealings with their enemies, show-ing no compunction or mercy as they tortured, raped, pillaged, and slaughtered. Templars weren't a group of "kind Christians"; rather, they showed the fanaticism of their faith by dealing out atrocities with the best of them. Out of the necessity of maintaining order as they grew in number, they starting admitting members with very questionable backgrounds. Many were outright criminals who wanted redemption as promised by the Church for fighting in Holy Wars. And most of the members were uneducated and often just men who unquestioningly followed the orders of their superiors—many to their death in supposed martyrdom.

Yet the order will always have its legacy in the secrets that it held through the tumultuous times in which it existed. I feel that the truth will eventually come out through the discovery of religious relics that have yet to be found. It will certainly rock our world, but when religion builds power and wealth on lies and deception, they'll eventually have to pay the piper.

Francine says that many of the surviving Templars were indeed assimilated into other orders, while some went into different secret societies, and still others went underground to continue their activities in secret. She claims that many have reincarnated into our present-day world and are actively working to give us the truth about Christ, spurred on by their past-life memories. She also states that the formation of the Knights Templar is very close to the rendition Sandy Hamblett gives in *The Templar Papers* (compiled and edited by Oddvar Olsen). Therefore, for those of you who would like to read more on the subject, this book is a good place to start.

CHAPTER 7

THE KNIGHTS
OF MALTA

*T*he secret society that became known as "the Knights of Malta" is a religious order of the Catholic Church that was formerly recognized by the pope in A.D. 1113. It was originally founded as a monastic Hospitaller order (and still exists in this form today) by Brother Gerard (also known as Blessed Gerard), who was serving with other brothers at a hospice in Jerusalem.

At the time, different orders of monks—such as the Benedictines, who formed the Knights Hospitaller, which was initially founded as a nursing order in Jerusalem— had their members train as warrior knights. By the middle of the 12th century, the Hospitaller order was clearly divided into two groups: those who worked with the sick and those who were members of the military. Thus, the Knights Hospitaller became a military order that defended pilgrims journeying to the Holy Land along with the Knights Templar. It then evolved into a very powerful Christian group whose members distinguished themselves in battle with the Muslims for control of Jerusalem and the Holy Land, and their soldiers wore a black surcoat with this symbol:

Brother Gerard initially acquired money and territories for the order from Jerusalem and outlying lands, but since the Knights Hospitaller was still considered a religious order, it was granted special privileges by the pope. For example, members were only subject to the authority of the Papacy, weren't required to pay any tithes, and were allowed property and buildings. At the height of the Kingdom of Jerusalem, the order held some 140 estates in the area and 7 great forts.

When Acre was captured by the Muslims in 1291, the presence of Christianity was ousted in the Holy Land, so Brother Gerard's order sought refuge in Cyprus. Not wanting to become involved in the turbulence of that area's politics, however, they sought a more permanent home and captured the island of Rhodes in 1309. When the Knights Templar were persecuted and had their holdings confiscated by the Catholic Church and King Philip the Fair in 1312, much of their property was given to the Knights Hospitaller (known at that point as "the Order of Rhodes"). Then, land in Spain, England, France, Germany, and Italy came into their possession, causing the monastic order to become wealthier than it had ever been. It was also forced to become more militaristic in nature, as members were fighting Barbary pirates constantly, along with invasions by the Sultan of Egypt in 1444, Mehmed II in 1480, and Suleiman in 1522.

When the order was defeated by Suleiman, members of the Knights Hospitaller were allowed to retreat to Sicily. After wandering in different parts of Europe for about seven years, they were granted a presence in Malta in 1530 by King Charles I of Spain, with the permission of the King of Sicily. The order then became known as "the Knights of Malta," even though they moved their headquarters to Rome in 1834 (where it exists today). This was partially because Napoleon captured Malta in 1798, and although deposed, the group kept its name by becoming "the Sovereign Military Order of Malta."

With the advent of the Reformation, Protestant states such as Germany (under Lutherans) and England (under King Henry VIII) confiscated many of the Knights of Malta's holdings, thereby decreasing their wealth drastically. After their defeat by Napoleon, they were basically in a state of flux until they were reorganized and granted "grand master" status by the pope in 1879. (A grand master is recognized as a head of state and has the ecclesiastical ranking of a cardinal, as far as the Church is concerned.)

It was also during this time of turmoil that the branch known as the "Most Venerable Order of St. John of Jerusalem" was formed. This Protestant offshoot of the Knights of Malta was recognized by the Catholic order in 1963. It's also interesting to note that both orders have sovereignty and were given observer status at the United Nations. This means that they can issue passports for diplomatic immunity, which they frequently do.

Questionable Ties and Practices

What makes the Knights of Malta a secret society is their allegiance to the Papacy. And although the Knights of Malta claim that they're an organization for everyone, only lesser membership is granted to laypeople. To be an elite member, you must be Catholic and show a royal bloodline for at least 100 years.

Many of the Knights of Malta's alliances and actions in the past and present are clandestine in nature, mostly due to their being controlled by the Vatican. For example, the order was linked with the "rat run," the post–World War II escape route that enabled high-ranking Nazis and German scientists to evade war-crime trials. Rumor has it that some of these criminals were issued "Sovereign Knight of Malta" passports that allowed them to escape to the Americas out of Germany. Reinhard Gehlen, Hitler's Eastern Front intelligence chief, was even decorated by the order, receiving the "Grand Cross of Merit."

The Knights of Malta are known to be anticommunist because of their Catholic and aristocratic roots. This stance has led to their strong ties with the CIA and their involvement in the cold war with Russia. In fact, one of the founding fathers of the CIA, William "Wild Bill" Donovan, was awarded the "Grand Cross of the Order of St. Sylvester," by Pope Pius XII. This is a prestigious papal knighthood and the highest Catholic award ever received by an American.

Yet the influence of the Knights of Malta is strongest in Latin America and Africa. Their membership has included individuals such as Nazi escapee Otto "Scarface" Skorzeny, who later settled in Spain with the help of dictator Francisco Franco; Juan Perón, the president and dictator of Argentina, whom recent CIA documents prove was involved in the laundering of Nazi gold through the Vatican Bank; General Augusto Pinochet of Chile, who is known to have killed and tortured thousands of Chileans in his reign of terror; and Count Umberto Ortolani, the Knights' ambassador to Uruguay, who is generally considered to be the brains of the infamous P2 Lodge, which has many former Nazi and fascist members.

Knights of Malta members have had other alliances of a questionable nature with the help of high-ranking members of the Catholic Church and the Vatican. For example, Joseph Retinger, one of the founders of the Bilderberg Group, was a former Knight of Malta and agent of the Vatican. Cardinal Francis Spellman of New York was purportedly directly involved in the 1954 military coup in Guatemala that murdered thousands, and in which the CIA has admitted complicity. Spellman has also been linked to the South American P2 group through his long involvement with acknowledged member Archbishop Paul Marcinkus, who headed the Vatican Bank and was believed to have numerous illegal dealings, which many officials wanted to question him about. He was never brought in, since being a Vatican employee gave him immunity.

Marcinkus was also suspected of being part of the plot that caused the death of Pope John Paul I. The pontiff's passing was very suspicious and led to the theory that he was poisoned, which the Church quickly hushed up. Many thought he was killed because he was too honest and wanted the Church to become more ecumenical in nature, but there's also the possibility that he knew too much about the illegal goings-on of the Vatican Bank. Cardinal Spellman was also an old friend of Wild Bill

Donovan, who was believed to be the head of the Knights of Malta in America for almost three decades.

The Knights of Malta are now very much involved in trying to get Europe to accept one president, as is evinced by the efforts of member and former president of the French Republic, Valéy Giscard d'Estaing, which are now backed by Britain, France, Germany, Italy, and Spain. In fact, many of these so-called medieval religious secret societies are working strongly in today's political realm. That's because in the Middle Ages the world was basically ruled by royalty and religion, while nowadays politics and money are in control. Many of these covert organizations just follow the power trail . . . and that's how they stay alive.

CHAPTER 8

THE ROSICRUCIAN ORDER

*A*s I begin this chapter, I'd like to impart some personal observations about the Rosicrucian Order. Although I'm not one of their members, I've always admired this group, and when I've gone to Egypt on my sponsored tours, it's amazing how many Rosicrucians have gone with me. I guess it makes sense, since a lot of the original members of this secret society were Gnostics and keepers of their mysterious knowledge (I'll talk more about this in Chapter 15).

The largest of the modern-day Rosicrucian Orders is "the Ancient Mystical Order Rosae Crucis (AMORC)," which has its headquarters in San Jose, California. Since I live in the same city, I know firsthand that these headquarters also include a planetarium and an Egyptian museum that my children and grandchildren love to visit.

Now the AMORC claims no religious affiliation and says that their beliefs don't interfere with any faith. I imagine that this would depend on interpretation because their teachings do relate to the areas of self-improvement and enlightenment; and I know that certain fundamentalist and right-wing type churches wouldn't be too pleased with subjects such as reincarnation, soul or astral travel, parapsychology, meditation, and the like. Of course to someone like me, it's not a problem. I think the AMORC has a good curriculum, but then I'm not conservative in my beliefs—I certainly preach religious tolerance and believe in reincarnation and the survival of the soul. After all, I'm a Gnostic, and that's what we do.

The Order's Background

The beginnings of the Rosicrucian movement are generally thought to be in either the 15th or 17th centuries, although some believe that their beginnings date all the way back to ancient Egyptian times. Regardless of when it actually started, its origins are steeped in mystery. According to the most popular legend, this group came about thanks to a monk named Christian Rosenkreuz, who was born in Germany in 1378. At the tender age of 16, he traveled to Damascus, Egypt, and Morocco, where he supposedly was tutored by Islamic masters of the occult arts. He then returned to Germany and is said to have begun the Rosicrucian Order with three monks from the original cloister that had raised him. Rosenkreuz expanded the membership to eight monks and built the *Spiritus Sanctum* (or "the House of the Holy Spirit"), which was completed in 1409.

The Spiritus Sanctum became Rosenkreuz's tomb when he died in 1484 at the age of 106. Knowledge of the tomb was then lost for about 120 years—it was rediscovered in the year 1604, which supposedly led to a resurrection of the Rosicrucian Order. The renewed interest has been attributed to the works of a German Lutheran pastor by the name of Johann Valentin Andrae (1586–1654). Evidently, Andrae wanted to create a group dedicated to social-life reformation, so he published three documents describing the Rosicrucian legend: *The Fama Fraternitas of the Meritorious Order of the Rosy Cross* (1614), *The Confession of the Rosicrucian Fraternity* (1615), and *The Chemical Marriage of Christian Rosenkreuz* (1616)—which was supposedly written by Christian Rosenkreuz himself in 1459.

This is where controversy starts to rear its head, for modern Rosicrucian groups have different opinions about the story of Rosenkreuz. Some believe that he existed as the above documents assert, others see the story as a parable that indicates more profound truths, and still others believe that Christian Rosenkreuz is a pseudonym for one or more historic personages (whom most believe to be Francis Bacon). While no one can come up with definitive proof of whether Rosenkreuz actually existed, the three documents published by Andrae had an almost instantaneous and profound effect. Rosicrucian societies arose quickly, and the rose-and-cross symbol became very popular (it may very well have come from Andrae's coat of arms, which purportedly has a similar image).

Along with the legend of Christian Rosenkreuz, there was a lesser-known myth put forth by a Rosicrucianist-Masonic group known as "Golden and Rosy Cross" in the 18th century that also described the order's beginnings. In this version, the movement began in the year A.D. 46, led by an Alexandrian Gnostic sage named Ormus. He and his six followers were evidently converted to Christianity by the disciple Mark; thus, Rosicrucianism was formed by combining Christianity with ancient Egyptian and Gnostic mysteries. Still others think that the sect started with the pharaoh Akhenaton in ancient Egypt.

However, Rosenkreuz is acknowledged by most Rosicrucians as their founder. When his rediscovered tomb was opened in 1604, many documents of ancient wisdom were purportedly found, which are allegedly used even to this day in the order's teachings. On his trip to the Middle East and Africa, Rosenkreuz reportedly studied alchemy, astrology, magic, exorcism, the Kabbalah, and other mystical subjects. He also examined the Pythagorean tradition of envisioning objects and ideas in terms of their numeric aspects. He supposedly also learned Divine and angelic names and was anointed as a master by Islamic mystics.

The Rosicrucian Order spread throughout Europe like wildfire, garnering advocates such as Englishman Robert Fludd (1574–1637)—who was also an alleged Grand Master of the Priory of Sion—who subsequently published *A Compendius Apology for the Fraternity of the Rosy Cross;* and Michael Maier (1568–1622), a physician of alchemy who helped merge that practice into the group's philosophy. Consequently, Rosicrucians supposedly demonstrated their ability to have healing powers, which they deemed to be a gift from God.

The Rosicrucians were certainly magnanimous as far as acquiring knowledge was concerned. They seem to have gleaned parts of their teachings and philosophy from Buddhism, Christianity, Gnosticism, Hinduism, Hermetic philosophy, and Islamic magic and esoteric teachings, along with the Kabbalah.

They also had some interaction with and effect on Freemasonry, as is indicated by their symbol being found in certain rituals of the Craft or Blue Lodges. In fact, the structure of the Rosicrucians is similar to that of Freemasonry in that they have different levels of advancement in secret knowledge. In my research, I also found them linked to the Illuminati and the Priory of Sion. And around 1530 (more than 80 years before the publication of the first manifesto of the Rosicrucians), it's documented that the rose and cross had already been found in Portugal in the Convent of the Order of Christ, home of the Knights Templar (which survived in Portugal as "the Order of Christ").

⁓

The Rosicrucian Order is considered to be an "inner world" group that contains what they call great "Adepts," whose knowledge, power, and wisdom almost make them demigods in comparison to ordinary men. They also have what is known as "the College of Invisibles," which is regarded as the source of the information behind the Rosicrucian movement. The group certainly believes in esoteric learning and utilizes a sacred astrology and other methods in order to obtain spiritual development and self-knowledge. Members believe that only two ways lead to Divine freedom: knowledge and love. They feel that the whole meaning of the universe is explained in their symbol—as with the rose blooming in the middle of the cross, humans must develop the capacity for love to the point where they care for all creatures, comprehend the laws that govern the world, and are able to proceed through intuition and the loving intelligence of the heart from every cause to every effect.

In the 18th century, the organized lodges of the Rosicrucian Order had elaborate rituals of admission, and it was also at this time that they were considered to be the most secret. Some of the symbols used in their rituals were:

- A glass globe standing on a pedestal that had seven steps and was divided into two parts representing light and darkness

- Three candelabras placed in a triangular format

- Nine glasses symbolizing male and female properties

- A brazier

- A circle

- A napkin

An initiate faced the usual symbolic death and rebirth ritualistic procedure and agreed to support his brethren and lead a virtuous life.

Because their beliefs draw upon other groups so much, it's hard to pin down this order's specific tenets, but they seem to have a lot of Gnosticism in them, as well as the positive parts of other philosophies. I didn't find that they're keeping any hidden knowledge that couldn't be obtained elsewhere, and they seem to be more interested in just living by their own rules and bettering themselves through learning. And, there doesn't seem to be any mention of a New World Order or getting into politics. If anything, they appear to be more involved in the arts, music, and literature; and they just keep to themselves and practice their own beliefs. I believe that the Rosicrucian Order is a good and upstanding organization as it exists today.

CHAPTER 9

THE PRIORY OF SION

*O*ne of the secret societies that's come to the public's attention thanks to the great success of *The Da Vinci Code* is the Priory of Sion. Some naysayers claim that the group doesn't even exist, but history—and I—beg to differ. As we've already learned, there was a Catholic monastic order in Jerusalem at the same time as the Knights Templar. This has been proven by the existence of a papal bull stating that this order had monasteries and abbeys at Mt. Carmel in Palestine, as well as properties in southern Italy and France. And an organization called the Priory of Sion registered with the bureau of records in Annemasse, France, in 1956.

Any problems that people have in accepting the existence of the Priory of Sion stem directly from one man, Pierre Plantard, who seems to have lied his way across Europe. He was reported to be a Nazi sympathizer and anti-Semite, boasted of being friends with many prominent people, and was supposed to be secretary-general and then a grand master of the Priory of Sion. It's this last claim that got Plantard in a lot of trouble.

While Plantard was serving the Priory in the 1960s, he appears to have forged documents that alluded to the survival of the sacred bloodline of the Merovingians, a line of Frankish kings. These documents, in turn, were used as part of the research for the book *Holy Blood, Holy Grail*. When authors Michael Baigent, Richard Leigh, and Henry Lincoln published their work in 1982, it immediately became a bestseller and stirred up worldwide controversy over its premise that there's a lineage still existing today that stems directly from Jesus Christ.

Holy Blood, Holy Grail caused such a sensation when it came out that it was subsequently put on the banned list by the Catholic Church. Dan Brown's *The Da Vinci Code* (a novel inspired by the premise of Baigent, Leigh, and Lincoln's nonfiction work) and other books followed, all of which put forth the controversial theory that Jesus Christ's descendants have survived to this day and that the Priory of Sion kept that secret. Unfortunately, when Plantard ultimately admitted that he forged the documents because he wanted to create the illusion that he, too, was part of the Merovingian line, scholars then turned on *Holy Blood, Holy Grail* because it utilized resources that have more or less been proven to be false. *The Da Vinci Code* has also been widely attacked, and several books have been written that attempt to debunk its whole premise.

So you'd think that this whole affair about Jesus having kids would go away, right? Well, it hasn't—and, in fact, it's gotten even more popular! A large part of this is due to the publicity that the brouhaha has raised, which has caused Christian scholars to come out of the woodwork in droves to defend what they feel is an attack on the Catholic Church, Christianity, and Jesus Christ himself. (What's that old saying from *Hamlet:* "The lady doth protest too much, methinks"?)

In the course of this international fervor, many examined the Priory of Sion documents that had been found, and they ended up contacting Pierre Plantard . . . who was only too eager to talk. Almost as soon as Plantard asserted that he was part of the Merovingian bloodline, his claims were proven to be false—and to make matters worse, he ultimately admitted that he and an accomplice had forged the documents Baigent, Leigh, and Lincoln discovered to substantiate his claim to the bloodline. Plantard resigned as grand master of the Priory of Sion in 1984 after suffering public humiliation, and died in February 2000. One might think that the controversy over this order would subside with Plantard's confession, but it roared back thanks to *The Da Vinci Code* and hasn't died down since.

One of the reasons why the controversy still exists is the fact that although the documents Baigent, Leigh, and Lincoln found in the National Library in Paris are readily accepted as being forged by Plantard, there seems to be some truth in them . . . and that thread leads to the Order of Sion, which existed in the 12th century. Now where did Plantard get the information to make his forgeries? Does anyone really think that a rascal such as Pierre Plantard would devote so much time to this incredibly intricate plot when he had no knowledge that it would ever come to light? If the authors of *Holy Blood, Holy Grail* hadn't discovered the documents, would they still be in the National Library gathering dust? Does the Priory of Sion still exist today, and if so, was all the hubbub over Plantard a smoke screen to cover their activities? Conspiracy theorists think so, and they continue to keep this hotly contested subject alive.

In my research, I discovered that Napoleon had ransacked the Vatican and taken boxes of information and treasure back to France. Although the French government reportedly returned some of it, they still kept countless so-called hidden or secret documents. This could very well be the explanation for why the Priory of Sion documents were in the National Library of France in the first place. Pierre Plantard's confession that he planted them there always seemed a little suspicious to me, especially when you consider the fact that he was facing a number of criminal charges—so he could very well have falsely confessed either for publicity or to escape criminal prosecution.

Here's What We Do Know

So here's a refresher course on what we do know about the Order of Sion (which I touched on in Chapter 6). A conclave of Calabrian monks left the Belgian Abbey of Orval in 1090 to journey to the Holy Land as pilgrims. Five years later, the first Crusade was launched, which ended with the capture of Jerusalem from the Muslims in 1099. One of the key players in the success of this venture was Godfrey of Bouillon, the devout knight from France whom I mentioned earlier. If you recall, after the capture of Jerusalem, the group of Calabrian monks and others elected Godfrey as *de facto* king of Jerusalem, but he refused the title and instead accepted that of "Protector of the Holy Sepulchre." He then founded a group of 12 knights called "the Order of the Holy Sepulchre," which eventually evolved into the Knights Templar (again, see Chapter 6).

Due to the Calabrian monks' support of Godfrey, which was based on the belief that he was a descendant of the Merovingians—and therefore also a descendant of King David through Jesus and Merovech—he made a place for the monks in an abbey on Mount Zion. Somewhere between 1099 and 1118, it's believed that this group of monks (now called the Order of Sion) and the men who would later be known as the Knights Templar became one organization and unified with the same leadership. There's no written documentation of this happening, but the Order of Sion did occupy an abbey on Mount Zion until about 1291, when Jerusalem was recaptured by Muslims. Mount Zion is also where the Knights Templar made their headquarters.

While there's some dispute as to when the Knights Templar was actually founded, it was formally recognized by the pope in 1139; and according to *Holy Blood, Holy Grail,* the Templars and the Order of Sion remained allied until an event called "the cutting of the elm" at Gisors in 1188. The history of the Templars also refers to the symbolic cutting of the elm, and the first grand master of the Priory of Sion is listed as Jean de Gisors, who was master of the castle and lands where this incident took place. I doubt that this is a coincidence.

The parting of the Order of Sion and the Knights Templar was evidently not acrimonious, for they purportedly stayed in contact with each other for centuries afterward. It's further believed that these two organizations shared much in the way of information and knowledge and had constant communication with each other even after they separated from one another. After vacating their abbey in Jerusalem, the Order of Sion seems to have existed for several hundred years until it was finally absorbed by the

Jesuits in the 17th century. It's interesting to note that in the 18th century, the Jesuits were suppressed by the Catholic Church, and this continued until their restoration in 1814. Now could this have been due to the influence of the absorbed Order of Sion?

I remember when I was studying theology in college and I learned about the suppression of the Jesuits and their danger of being excommunicated from the "Mother Church." Then all of a sudden they were let back in and accepted. Could this be because they knew too much and it was a case of "keep your friends close but keep those who know too much even closer"? The Jesuits are usually very scholarly and brilliant, and I'm sure to this day they know more than they'll ever reveal.

There are also several links between the Order of Sion, which was made up of Calabrian monks, and the Carmelites. For example, Saint Berthold, the founder of the Carmelites, originated from Calabria. Fra Lippi, a tutor of Botticelli's, lived in Calabria and was known as "the Carmelite." Saint Thérèse of Lisieux turns up in a number of the order's churches, as well as her namesakes: Teresa of Avila, a Carmelite and mystic, and Mother Therese of St. Augustine, a Carmelite nun who was murdered by zealots during the French Revolution. (I'm very close to the Carmelites because of my dear friend Sister Emmanuel, who's a member of their convent in Spokane, Washington.)

There's some evidence that after the cutting of the elm, the Order of Sion then either became the Priory of Sion or had an internal division that resulted in the Priory. According to *The International Encyclopedia of Secret Societies and Fraternal Orders* by Alan Axelrod, there were nine grades to the Priory of Sion, which divided into different "levels" or "provinces" that were very close to how the Knights Templar's internal structure was ordered. Due to the fact that they resided together and had the same leadership for a number of years, this just gives more of an indication that the two organizations were closely linked. There are also Masonic overtones in both groups' structure, so it's very possible that these were taken from the Priory by the Masons, although this remains to be proven. While some researchers have said that the Priory of Sion had its beginnings in pagan beliefs, history shows that it was avowedly Catholic, although it differed with the Church in many areas of dogmatic belief.

According to the documents discovered in the National Library in Paris, the long list of grand masters of the Priory includes some very famous people. Among those listed were René d'Anjou, Nicholas Flamel, Sandro Filipepi (better known as Botticelli, the renowned Renaissance painter), Leonardo da Vinci, Robert Fludd, Johann Valenin Andrea, Robert Boyle, Isaac Newton, Charles Radclyffe, Charles de Lorraine, Charles Nodier, Victor Hugo, Claude Debussy, and Jean Cocteau.

It's interesting to note that Leonardo da Vinci seems to have had a "thing" for John the Baptist. In addition, there are indications that the Priory of Sion and the Knights Templar were also interested highly in "Johannism" (the belief that John was the true Messiah and Jesus a false one, although some do believe that they were co-Messiahs). Supposedly every grand master in the Priory takes the name *Jean* (French for "John") as an honoree title to represent John the Baptist. I personally think that this is a nod to their early roots in the Jewish Christian (or Gnostic) philosophy.

The Hunchback Allegory

I think you might find the following very intriguing. In the course of researching this book, I kept coming across Victor Hugo's name, mostly relating to the Priory of Sion.

As many of you know, my background is in literature and theology; and Victor Hugo, of course, wrote the famous novel *The Hunchback of Notre Dame. Notre Dame* means "our lady," and it's interesting to note that Hugo picked this church for his story, possibly giving a tip of his hat to Mary Magdalene, since he was purportedly a grand master in the Priory of Sion. If you begin to "think outside the box," his story takes on a whole new symbolic meaning. In fact, it seems that many of these famous writers held secrets that they camouflaged in their writings with symbolism or clues. . . .

If you haven't read Hugo's book, you can get the gist of the story from the film starring Charles Laughton and Maureen O'Hara. It's a very good movie, but it's better if you read the tale because it will reveal more secrets about Notre Dame. For the sake of this chapter, however, I'll provide a brief outline of the book's main points.

This is a story about a child left on the doorstep of the Notre Dame cathedral because of his deformity. He's adopted by a supposedly kind bishop and grows up to be Quasimodo, a grotesque hunchback with a great heart. He's allowed to stay in Notre Dame to ring the bells, which also makes him deaf. His only home is the church, and from its high parapets he sees this beautiful girl, Esmeralda, and falls in love. Even though he realizes it's hopeless because of his ugliness, he still loves her from afar.

Now could it be that Victor Hugo thinly veils what's ugly and concealed in the Catholic Church by putting it in the guise of a deformed and deaf hunchback who has to stay hidden because the populace at this time was so superstitious that any abnormality was thought to be evil? Esmeralda, representing innocence (and also a symbol for Mary Magdalene or even the feminine principle of the Mother God), is lusted after by the bishop, who tries to have her kidnapped by Quasimodo. That plot fails, and Quasimodo is caught and disciplined. During his punishment, Esmeralda offers him water out of sympathy, which endears her more to the hunchback. Overcome with lust, the bishop stabs one of Esmeralda's suitors yet accuses her of attempted murder, so she's convicted and sentenced to hang. The hunchback rescues her from the hanging and takes her to the bell tower and claims "sanctuary" (protection of the church) for her.

Doesn't this smack of a complete analogy of what was happening in the Church at the time? The public didn't know (or even think about) the truth as far as the Church was concerned, so Hugo tried to tell them that "things are not always what they seem."

Later on in the story, the bishop is again rejected by Esmeralda, and he arranges to remove sanctuary to give her back to the people to be hanged. After Quasimodo tries to protect her, Esmeralda is eventually executed, and he sees the bishop for what he is. Quasimodo throws the bishop off the top of the bell tower to his death and then locks himself in Esmeralda's tomb and dies . . . not a happy ending.

Most literary scholars give the book high acclaim for its passion, especially as a lesson to be kinder to those less fortunate, yet no one seems to see how glaring the truth is. Hugo put many clues in this book: the sanctimonious bishop who was ravaged by lust and power (the Catholic Church); the innocence of the girl (Mary Magdalene); the deformed hunchback (the ugliness hidden within the Church); and the hunchback throwing the bishop off the tower (the triumph of the truth over the Church's lies).

Hugo tried to couch the fact that the outward appearance of the Church doesn't represent its reality in any way. He was attempting to impart a message that maybe only the Priory of Sion knew, but like Leonardo da Vinci, he hoped that someday someone would see through this veil of symbolism to unearth the secrets the Church was hiding.

The Rennes-le-Chateau Mystery

Here's another mysterious story that I think you'll find interesting. In 1885, Father Berenger Sauniere was assigned to the parish at Rennes-le-Chateau in southern France, the church of which had been dedicated to Mary Magdalene in 1059 (possibly due to the fact that many believed she'd lived there after the Crucifixion). I find it a minor miracle that *any* religious building was dedicated to her, especially when you realize that the Catholic Church held her in such low esteem at that time.

As the story goes, Father Sauniere was very poor until about 1887, when he reputedly found either one or four (accounts differ) hidden document(s) in a hollow pillar within the church. After reading the material, he began excavations inside the church and supposedly deciphered an encrypted inscription on the tomb of Marie de Negre d'Ables, Lady of Blanchfort, in the graveyard outside the church. Afterward, he traveled to Carcassonne and talked to the deputy of the bishop who resided there.

After that consultation, the fortunes of Father Sauniere immediately turned. He received vast amounts of money and began to refurbish the church in an ornate, almost garish, style. Many wonder why he renovated the church the way he did. Over the porch lintel is the bizarre inscription: "This Place Is Terrible"; a statue of the demon Asmodeus "guards" the door; and the plaques depicting the Stations of the Cross contain strange changes from the norm, such as a child swaddled in Scottish plaid, Pontius Pilate wearing a veil, St. Joseph and Mary each holding a Christ child (as if to imply that the son of God had a twin), and Jesus being carried to (or from?) his tomb at night.

The big question, however, was how Sauniere got all this money. Some say that he obtained it by "selling" masses (an act of indulgence frowned upon by the Church). Well, such sales *were* a lucrative practice for many priests, but Sauniere's parish was very poor and he didn't travel much, so where would the affluent patrons have come from? The amount of wealth he accumulated in such a short period of time points to another source. Is it a coincidence that he got very rich just after his visit to his superiors? Did he discover some big secret and blackmail the religious authorities, or did he find a treasure while he was excavating the parish church? The priest refused to reveal the source of his fortune to anyone other than his housekeeper of many years, who had a stroke and died without ever being able to reveal the secret.

When Father Sauniere himself passed away in 1917, many said that he'd been blackmailing the Catholic Church because upon hearing his confession on his deathbed, the priest attending him refused to give him absolution or the last rites. The source of Sauniere's instant wealth has never been explained to anyone's great satisfaction and remains a mystery today. (The irony of all this is that he evidently spent everything he obtained, for he died in poverty.)

The Rennes-le-Chateau area has become a huge tourist attraction thanks to Father Sauniere. Other mysteries also intrigue visitors, such as:

- Did Mary Magdalene live in the area, and is she buried there?

- Did Christ live with her there, and is he also buried there?

- Is there a great Knights Templar treasure there, and did Sauniere find it?

Pierre Plantard tied the Priory of Sion to Rennes-le-Chateau in his documents, but if they were forged, you can't really place much substance in this. The only link that I could find with the Order of Sion concerned the Knights Templar, as they did control that area for a time. Also, after the elm-cutting incident (which I mentioned earlier in this chapter) that basically split them into two separate societies, some have postulated that the Templars were very busy with increasing their wealth and holdings, while the Order of Sion was more "spiritually" following their original combined agenda, although no one really knows for certain. Therefore, the Rennes-le-Chatueau mystery remains cloaked in secrecy for the time being.

Where There's Smoke, There's Fire

Humankind certainly does have a yen for secrets. After all, a good whodunit and its ultimate solution has created a whole genre of suspense books that are avidly read across the globe. If the populace is exposed to a real-life thriller, they'll eat it up! Such is what is occurring around the world now. From the mystery of Father Berenger Sauniere and Rennes-le-Chateau to the little Rosslyn chapel near Edinburgh, Scotland, with its marvelous Templar artwork, along with purported codes in Leonardo da Vinci's artwork and churches and cathedrals throughout Europe, Dan Brown and other writers have created one of the biggest controversies of the modern age . . . one that has the whole planet salivating for more. My grandmother used to say that if there's smoke, there's usually a fire. Well, there certainly has been enough smoke here that we're sure to find the blaze that was sparked by the Priory of Sion.

I commented earlier that what makes the study of all of these secret societies and the knowledge they hold extremely difficult is that there have been so many offshoots of the original groups over the years, and that these societies overlap constantly. The Priory of Sion, Knights Templar, Cathars, Rosicrucians, and Freemasons are all interlinked; in fact, you find instances of members of these organizations having contact and interaction with each other over and over again.

The supposed grand masters of the Priory of Sion were heavily involved with the aforementioned societies. For example, I found that Robert Fludd was a leading exponent of esoteric thought and was allegedly one of the men most responsible for bringing Rosicrucianism to

England. Both Robert Boyle and Isaac Newton were heavily involved in alchemy and were confidants. Charles Radclyffe promoted the "Scottish Rite" of Freemasonry and was close friends with Andrew Ramsay, who was also a good pal of Newton's. Charles de Lorraine was the first European prince to become a Mason. Charles Nodier was the mentor for Victor Hugo, Honoré de Balzac, and others who drew upon esoteric and Hermetic tradition. Claude Debussy was an integral member of the symbolist circles that also included Oscar Wilde, W. B. Yeats, and Marcel Proust. And Jean Cocteau was associated with royalist Catholic circles, but his redecoration of churches reflected Rosicrucian themes. All of these individuals were not only past grand masters of the Priory of Sion, but were also involved with esoteric philosophies and the societies that promulgated them (Rosicrucians, Freemasonry, and so on).

I'm not convinced that the Priory of Sion exists today as the group that Pierre Plantard put forth. Its goals or agenda may still live on with some other organization or secret society, but I believe that its members were in fact absorbed by the Jesuits around 1617 or so. If the Priory had survived to the present day, it would surely have had to branch out as an extremely clandestine sect that's perhaps operating under a different name.

~

CHAPTER 10

OPUS DEI

$\mathcal{F}$ounded in 1928 in Madrid, Spain, by the Roman Catholic priest Josemaria Escriva, Opus Dei is a Catholic organization whose mission is to spread the word that everyone is called to become a saint and apostle of Jesus Christ and that life is a path to sanctity. The group's formal name is "Prelature of the Holy Cross and Opus Dei," but it's commonly known just as *Opus Dei*, which is Latin for "a work of God."

Years after its founding, Opus Dei was established as a personal prelature by Pope John Paul II, thus making it a part of the Church's institutional structure. In fact, many Catholic leaders support what they see as the group's innovative teachings—along with its complete fidelity to the Church—through which it is able to (hopefully) solve the challenges of the world. Yet this society has often been accused of secrecy, ultraconservative beliefs, a right-wing political agenda, and even cultlike methods as far as how it treats its members.

As an aside, Amway and other multilevel marketing organizations, charismatics, and Pentecostals have also been listed as cults by some watchdog groups. This may seem ludicrous, but it appears that any sort of gathering, religious or not, can become a cult. It can happen anywhere, with even the best of intentions, when the human ego comes in and starts to complicate very simple teachings. Christianity is the greatest example of this—the religion doesn't actually follow Jesus Christ's words, but rather puts its own spin on them.

Anyway, Opus Dei came into the public's consciousness because of *The Da Vinci Code,* in which author Dan Brown calls it a "Catholic sect" on the novel's first page relating to "facts." Brown then spins a story in which the fanatical devotion of one of this group's members and the self-interest of its leader are used by a mysterious retainer for sinister motives. Brown has said that his portrayal of Opus Dei was based on interviews with current and former members, along with various books about the organization.

Of course we know that *The Da Vinci Code* stirred up a hornet's nest that has kept Opus Dei and the Vatican hopping to this day. In response to the controversy, Opus Dei spokesperson Marc Carrogio issued a "declaration of peace" to Brown and his publisher, while other Christian scholars deemed the work to be either willful ignorance or purposeful malice. I'd like to make one thing very clear here: I think that many people have totally forgotten that *this is a work of fiction!* We all need to remember that authors have freedom of speech and literary license to put forth their own points of view. Being a nonfiction writer myself, I've always tried my best to back up my words with evidence, but a novelist doesn't have to (although I think most do try to get their facts straight, and I include Mr. Brown in that category).

If you think that Opus Dei has been maligned, Dan Brown himself has attracted even more spite with a horde of books trying to debunk him and his work. Christian scholars and historians have come out of the woodwork with scathing criticisms of his writing and research, but I for one (along with millions of others, I might add) found *The Da Vinci Code* to be highly entertaining. While a work of fiction is often based on *some* facts, to expect a novelist to expend the time on research that a scholar does is ridiculous and should be seen as such. I've always found that people who are secure in their belief systems don't have to scream and criticize those who attack them, but those who are insecure in their faith always fight back—sometimes viciously.

What's This Society All About?

Vatican analyst John L. Allen, Jr., did some recent studies on Opus Dei because of the criticism it has received, and he concluded that some of the group's views are misunderstood due to their newness—yet he also said that Opus Dei was the most controversial force in the Catholic Church. And in 1994, Dr. Massimo Introvigne (a conservative Catholic scholar and socialist of religion) said that the organization was only a target because as a secular society they were "returning to religion." I really don't understand this for the simple reason that I don't believe religion ever left. I imagine this merely means that most secular societies practice religion in private, while Opus Dei is now "going public," so to speak.

I understand that when you come across some of these quotes from scholars and supposedly learned men, you may be left with the thought, *What in the hell does that mean?* For example, Pope John Paul II once declared:

"Opus Dei is an institution which has in fact striven not only to enlighten with new lights the mission of the laity in the Church and in society, but also to put it into practice. It has also striven to put into practice the teaching of the universal call to holiness, and to foster at all levels of society the sanctification of ordinary work, and these it does by means of ordinary work." If you're not confused by now, you sure are much, much smarter than I'll ever be!

Adding to the confusion is that while Opus Dei seems to want members of high academic ability, it also appears to believe in "family values" and the subjugation of women. Unquestioned obedience (very useful to totalitarian governments) and a great degree of regulating power for the Church are also part of their creed. What follows in italics are tenets that come directly from Opus Dei, while my two cents are added in parentheses:

1. Holiness in ordinary life: Having become members of God's family through baptism, all Christians are called to a life of holiness. (Which means that like so many religions, *theirs* is the only one. This isn't a criticism; it's just that every religion believes only it has the truth. Spirituality, on the other hand, instructs that everyone is allowed to believe in whatever they feel is best for them.)

2. Whatever work Christians do is done with a spirit of excellence as an effective service for the needs of society, working out of love for God and all men and women. (I believe this part, as long it doesn't come with a price. In other words, we should always do good, but not just by building big churches. Let's construct homes for the elderly, children, and the homeless instead—wouldn't this give real honor to God?)

3. Love for freedom: Christians should love personal freedom, both their own and that of all men and women. God the son himself, on becoming man took on human freedom. As man, he obeyed his Father's will throughout his whole life, even unto death. By his free-will choice, each person directs his life toward eternal union with God or eternal separation. (I believe that you choose your own road—whether it be hard, lonely, or easy—to glorify and learn for God, for we are part of Him. To that end, Jesus was actually preordained to fulfill his prophecy. I also don't believe that "eternal separation" exists, for in the end even the wicked will be absorbed back into our all-loving God.)

4. Prayer and mortification: Love the essence of sanctity in constant childlike prayer. (Prayer *is* powerful, but you can "live" prayer by doing good deeds.) *Read sacred scripture and give devotion to the Virgin Mary.* (What sacred scripture do they mean here? I assume that they're speaking of the Bible, but most researchers know that it was highly edited by the early Catholic Church, and I doubt whether followers of other religions would consider the Bible the only "holy scripture" there is. The early Church also designated Christ's birth as "virgin," but didn't recognize Mary in any holy capacity until the third Ecumenical Council in the year A.D. 431, when they proclaimed her

Theotokos, which means "God bearer," "Birth giver of God," or "Mother of God," depending upon how you want to translate it. The Church also took a long time to completely accept the "Immaculate Conception," which was finally done in 1854, and the "Assumption of Mary," which was done in 1950. In other words, even the Catholic Church had many debates on Mary.)

Mortification, "prayer of the senses," is especially done through a sporting struggle to practice all the human virtues out of love. (Some Opus Dei members are known to have practiced mortification—a form of penance by denial, lifestyle, or infliction of pain or bodily harm. They're certainly not alone, as many orders throughout history have denied themselves food; slept on the floor, hard beds, or even nails; worn hair shirts; lived in poverty; flagellated themselves; or worn instruments of torture. Through their suffering, they felt that they were giving homage to God by doing penance for their sinful ways. Some groups practice mortification even now, and it's a shame because Jesus always stressed that our bodies were temples of the Lord. I also don't believe that an all-loving God would feel that homage should be done in this way.)

5. Christians are to give the highest importance to the virtue of charity, understanding, compassion, courtesy, and helping the needy; leading people to God, the source of peace and joy. (I believe in all of this.)

6. Unity of life: A Christian who seeks God, not just in church, but also in the most material things, has no double life—a life of faith divorced from daily work. Instead, he has a unity of life. (I agree with this until materialism takes over a person's life. Also, Catholic dogma demands that you must go to church.)

Father James Martin, a Jesuit and associate editor of *America Magazine,* belittles the above maxims, stating, "They range from traditional Christian pieties to sayings that could have come out of *Poor Richard's Almanac.*" Of course there are always going to be naysayers, but it's unusual for one of the same faith to give out a criticism.

Nevertheless, John Allen, Jr., reports that despite the criticism of Opus Dei, the organization has about 90,000 members. He goes on to say, "At the level of overall impression, how one interprets the facts about Opus Dei seems to depend on one's basic approach to spirituality, family life, and religious vocation." Allen states that although Opus Dei is accused of high control of members through tight schedules and internal confessors, the vast majority of those he met were healthy, well adjusted, running their own lives, and no threat to themselves or others.

Most of Opus Dei's members are what they call "supernumeraries," which comprise about 70 percent of the organization. Supernumeraries are usually married men and women with families who have regular jobs, homes, and so forth and help Opus Dei when they can find time to do so. "Numeraries," which comprise less than 20 percent of the membership, are men and women who commit themselves to celibacy for apostolic reasons; are able to live in the centers of Opus Dei; and usually work full-time for the organization in teaching, administration, and the like. "Numerary assistants" is another membership classification, and these are women who do the domestic chores necessary at the various centers. Then there are the "associates," who seem to have some administrative capacity. And the young men chosen for the final membership classification of "clergy" tend to be chosen from the ranks of the numeraries or associates.

Although John Allen, Jr., states that Opus Dei's assets just in the United States are estimated at around $344 million, this is nothing in comparison to the annual revenue of the Catholic Church, which comes in at about $100 billion. Even though critics have charged that Opus Dei is very rich and uses its money to gain influence and political power, there aren't enough facts to support this.

A Critic Raises Some Concern

According to Alan Axelrod in *The International Encyclopedia of Secret Societies and Fraternal Orders,* "Opus Dei is unique within the Catholic Church as a personal prelature. This gives it a high degree of independence from local control by parishes or bishops and according to some writers, this degree of control has made Opus Dei in effect a secret society."

Critics allege that the agenda of Opus Dei is the introduction of an almost "medieval" form of Christianity and the support of reactionary governments and regimes, so long as they're nominally Catholic. One of the most probing analyses of the group comes from Michael Walsh in his book *Opus Dei: An Investigation into the Powerful Secretive Society Within the Catholic Church,* in which he links it to extreme right-wing political movements and the Vatican banking scandals of the 1980s. Walsh indicates that Opus Dei may have tried to buy respectability by pumping huge sums of money into the Vatican, and he also implicates them in numerous other scandals.

Another critic, Austrian Franz Schaefer, has made some points that are especially worth contemplating. Remember, this is one man's perception—I include it here because, as always, I want you to be able to make up your own mind.

Schaefer states that he's a communist and former practicing Catholic. His background includes work in computer science, and he currently runs his own Internet company. He's also been involved in many political activist groups in Europe and is known for his work in that arena. Many call him a devout enemy of Opus Dei, but after I read some of his work, I found him to be more of an open-minded skeptic. In fact, he raises some questions that I might very well have asked or commented on myself. I consider myself to be fairly open and tolerant about religion and politics, so his views don't bother me at all. (By the way, although I'm definitely not a communist, I do feel that the Western world has to get over our "McCarthy" image of what the party is like—times and values change, and the communists of today are not the same as those of the Stalin or Khrushchev eras.)

Franz Schaefer states in his paper on Opus Dei (**www. mond.at/~schaefer**) that anyone can copy his material, but that it's also a work in progress (sounds reasonable to me). He firmly believes that the organization is a fundamentalist sect that operates in a Catholic environment;

although the Church denies this, Schaefer says that if you read the material involved in the group's makeup, he has every confidence that you'll agree with him.

He's particularly critical about Opus Dei's founder, Father Josemaria Escriva, who was later made a saint by Pope John Paul II (in the face of much criticism, I might add). Schaefer says that Escriva had fascist leanings and a large ego, which is somewhat borne out by Maria del Carmen Tapia's book *Beyond the Threshold: A Life in Opus Dei.* According to Schaefer, Tapia claims that she worked closely with Escriva in Rome for a number of years before they had a falling out, and then she was locked up without any outside communication with the world (other than smuggled letters) for six months or so. Perhaps we can attribute Tapia's treatment as punishment for wrongdoing in Opus Dei or her book as a vengeful vendetta against the organization (as some do), but other things about Escriva—especially his writings, which form the cornerstone of the Opus Dei philosophy—do cause some concern.

For example, Schaefer claims there are fascist ideologies in Escriva's teachings, which are very fundamentalist and have no religious tolerance. The guidelines of Opus Dei and its founder, some of which are withheld from the public, also call for "blind obedience" from its members; and it's said that Escriva called his writings "The Work of God." Schaefer also indicates that the organization exerts psychological control of its members through weekly "chats" in which these individuals are encouraged to tell the innermost secrets about their lives.

Franz Schaefer's campaign on Opus Dei apparently started when a friend of his "got sucked up in the cult" (his words, not mine) and he searched the Internet for information on the group. He states that he found very little data (this must have been sometime ago, for there's tons of stuff out there now), so he started researching the subject because he didn't want anyone else falling into their traps.

Schaefer feels that the Church has gathered a lot of dogmatic dust that covers the message of Jesus, and with Catholicism's corrupt and bloody history, why should we believe that it's perfect now? (Given the recent scandals with child abuse and banking, I can see his point, but I also believe that there were even sects in Gnosticism that broke off and became very austere, celibate, and controlling—although usually these factions didn't last long and had no history of persecution.) He believes that Opus Dei misinterprets Christ's words for their own ends, and he's convinced that the group is successfully taking over the Catholic Church. He points out that there's less and less distinction between the two every day and that many powerful positions in the Church belong to members of Opus Dei.

Schaefer also thinks that the majority of those who join this organization are upright people with good hearts who love God and want to do beneficial things for Him. He states that these are usually important and intelligent individuals because they can increase Opus Dei's influence in society and are able to donate large sums of money, but they don't see the fascist overtones of Josemaria Escriva.

Franz Schaefer also says (and I believe) that we have to be discerning when it comes to religious teachings and that everything we can ask should have answers and be made accessible to the inquisitive mind. I also agree with him that if we don't use our intellect, we could join groups that take all our money or assets, elect messiahs, instruct us to commit suicide while waiting for a space-ship, control our lives and thoughts, and demand strict obedience.

I believe that if we use our rational minds, common sense, and innate feelings of what's right and wrong, then we're on track—and we mustn't sacrifice any of these things to *any* organization, no matter how "holy" it seems to be. That's why I always try to preface any lecture or written material with this premise: "Take with you what you want and leave the rest behind, otherwise you set yourself up (as so many do) as the only truth."

I agree with Mr. Schaefer that the elemental teachings of Jesus are constantly being interpreted in a manner that's expedient for whatever Christian churches want to accomplish. Thus the basic Gnostic message of "just do good works" seems to take a backseat to humankind's propensity to make things very complicated.

~~~

In Opus Dei they have the idea of "childhood in front of God," which I suppose means that we become childlike in trust and adoration of God. This is part of *The Way*, written by Father Escriva, which is the main foundation for the organization. Unfortunately, members have taken this premise to the point that they obey the group's leadership without question in all things and are in essence the followers of a dictatorship. They don't give any suggestions because they're not allowed to, and they're mandated to attend weekly sessions in which they have to tell the authorities their most private thoughts.

The reason why Opus Dei is often called fascist is because Josemaria Escriva was close friends with Spanish dictator Francisco Franco; and in *The Way,* it states that "everything should be under the control of the leader." This work also instructs: "You shall not buy books without the advice of an experienced Christian. [Who defines what or who is an experienced Christian? The clergy?] It is so easy to buy something useless or mischievous. Often people think they are carrying a book under their arm, but they only carry a book of mud."

In addition, Maria Tapia (remember her from earlier in this chapter?) claimed that Opus Dei reads members' private mail. In fact, she stated that she had to write reports on all the people in her weekly talk sessions and submit them to her superiors. Then they'd come back to her and tell her exactly what to say to particular members who had "spilled their guts" to her. They also supposedly have agents who lurk in public "chat rooms" on Websites.

I'm constantly amazed by the way people can be fooled into thinking that an organization like Opus Dei is "breaking new ground" in religion or in its teachings. Their concept of having laypeople living saintly lives as a "vocation" is certainly not new, as Jesus and other religious leaders taught this, although this bunch is what we might term "elitist" with their wealth and their promise of a better life in heaven. I certainly don't disagree with the latter part, but we must also realize we have to live in tolerance, be lawful, show kindness and love to our fellow human beings, and do as many good deeds as we can to help ourselves and others live in this negative plane.

This organization also exerts quite an influence in our everyday world: According to statistics submitted in 1979 by the then-head of the order, Opus Dei had members in 479 universities, 664 newspapers, 52 radio and TV stations, 38 news and advertising companies, and 12 movie-production companies. You can imagine how many members are in place in these areas now!

But Where's the Proof?

The bottom line is that Opus Dei is a very conservative religious organization, just as the Catholic Church is (which is why the very conservative Pope John Paul II liked it so much). And the group is just one of many secular organizations within the Church. What really bothers me about much of the information I've shared with you in this chapter is that there's so little concrete proof of anything evil or untoward on Opus Dei's part.

I guess I'm super sensitive because I myself have been subjected to Websites claiming that I'm dead, that I'm a millionaire, that I'm a fraud and scam artist and not psychic, and that I don't write my own books. The first and last are the easiest to prove: I'm obviously still alive, and I have the original copies of my books written in my own hand. As for the other claims, I earn decent money, but most of it goes into my church and salaries for my employees. Overall, although I'm not 100 percent accurate, my abilities are certainly not in question as far as the thousands of people I've counseled successfully are concerned.

I know firsthand that whenever someone is in the public eye, rumors and untruths fly like birds in the sky. So in defense of Opus Dei, its critics may have some truth, but as the old saying goes, you really can't believe all that you read or hear. I'm sure that the group has controls and rules. With any organization that large, you're going to have members who are unhappy. For these men and women, the truth is that the organization was not for them, so in their minds and hearts, they were treated in an objectionable manner.

ODAN (Opus Dei Awareness Network) is one of several associations that give help to former and present members, and it states that since 1991, they've been in contact with people all over the world who have been subjected to the order's questionable practices. ODAN has reportedly been in touch with former and present members; their parents, siblings, and friends; and priests, bishops, campus ministers, and news reporters from Catholic and secular press. From the contacts that ODAN has made, it's become apparent that wherever this personal prelature exists, controversy follows.

I'm not upholding or criticizing Opus Dei, but in my research I couldn't find anything linking them to cults or any evil, clandestine operation. Do they have secrets? I'm sure they do, just as the Knights Templar, Freemasons, and Skull and Bones do, but I couldn't find evidence that they perpetrated any ongoing nefarious acts . . . and their actions are certainly not on the level of some of the other secret societies. Yes, the founder of Opus Dei had a close relationship with Franco, but I didn't discover any evidence that went beyond that and could find very little political involvement in general. And yes, they'd like everyone to embrace Catholicism, but then again, what religion doesn't want to be the "only one"?

Unlike other covert groups, Opus Dei doesn't seem to be the guardian of any secrets such as the Knights Templar, Masons, and others do. They appear to be autonomous unto themselves and only interested in holy actions and works. Their methods may come into question with some who have experienced them; and like Scientology, Opus Dei is clearly not for everyone. Being conservative, they're going to try to exert as much control on a member as possible, feeling that they're right in doing so. So if you dislike being controlled, Opus Dei is definitely not for you.

In my research, I didn't find anything that points to a real threat such as a political or religious takeover (unlike other secret societies). I also feel that as long as people aren't being brainwashed or forced to do things against their will, aren't posing a threat, and are living in harmony (many of Opus Dei's members seem to be content with their works and celibacy), we should leave them to practice their religion on what they feel is their own road or path. After all, wasn't the U.S. founded on the principle of freedom of worship?

I find it not only amazing but even tragic that America's forefathers escaped from England in order to seek freedom from religious oppression, only to form groups that had far more regulations than what they escaped from. The Puritans, for example, were a harsh group by any standards—they were told how to dress and when to pray, women were to be obedient to their husbands, and so on. Humankind wants to be free and then turns around and imposes rules that are often more stringent than what came before.

There will always be a segment of our population for which these strict, controlling organizations are appealing, but I believe that most of us want the freedom to worship and love God in our own way. I guess we'll always have leaders and followers, so if you're guiding others, do so with love and no ego. And if you're relying upon the wisdom of someone "above" you, always be sure in your heart and mind that you're doing what's absolutely right for you. If there's any doubt at all, then you need to take a closer look at your choices.

PART III

THE
DARK SIDE
OF
SECRECY

CHAPTER 11

THE ILLUMINATI

*T*he term *illuminati*—meaning "enlightened ones" in Latin—has been appropriated by various organizations, some real and some fictitious. Today, however, it mainly refers to the Bavarian Illuminati, a secret society that allegedly has conspiratorial aims to destroy the national identities of countries and the Catholic Church in the hopes of establishing a New World Order (which I'll explain in more detail in the next chapter). But before we get into all of that, let's take a look at what little we know about the groups that have called themselves "illuminati" over the years.

The Birth of a Powerful Movement

While some associations used the name *illuminati* as far back as ancient Egyptian times, I'd like to focus on when it first appeared in the world of Christianity. "The Brethren of the Free Spirit" (who advocated that humans could do anything they wanted as long as their souls were above sin) used the term *illuminati* in the 14th century, as did the Alumbrados of Spain (who believed illumination came from within) in the 15th and 16th centuries. Yet even though these different groups may have used the term, they weren't the forerunners of the Bavarian Illuminati. Ironically enough, that honor seems to belong to an Islamic organization.

A powerful society that called itself *Roshaniya,* or "the illuminated ones," and was based on a secret cult started to rise in the mountains of Afghanistan in the 16th century. The Roshaniya were founded by a man named Bayezid Ansari, who claimed that his ancestors had aided Mohammed after his flight from Mecca. Because of that help, Ansari insisted that he'd been granted admission into the mysteries of the Ishmaelite religion—which involved a covert training that dated from Abraham's rebuilding of the Temple at Mecca.

Ansari started a school in which he instructed his initiates in the supernatural teachings of the Ishmaelite, and each candidate had to go through a form of probation that included periods of silent meditation known as *khilwat.* It was during these times of contemplation that an initiate was to receive the illumination that emanated from the group's supreme being . . . which involved directing the world through a class of perfect men and women.

Bayezid Ansari evidently received great support from merchants and soldiers who gave to his coffers and sustained his school, as well as the expensive but effective military and political espionage system he ran. As he became successful, Ansari started expressing the notion that there was no afterlife of the kind currently believed in; that is, there was no reward or punishment after death, only a state of spirit in which you could essentially "eat, drink, and be merry." Therefore, since he believed that there were no Divine consequences, he cultivated the aims of the Roshaniya to have power over the world by putting forth axioms such as: "Gain power, look after yourself"; "You have no allegiance except to the Order"; and "All humanity that cannot identify itself by our secret sign is our lawful prey."

The Mark of Adam Weishaupt

The secret order of the Roshaniya stayed in existence for more than 100 years. In 1776, approximately 40 years after the death of the order's last leader, a man by the name of Adam Weishaupt formed a similar group in Germany. Weishaupt was raised by Jesuits in a very conservative and Catholic-controlled part of that country and went on to become a professor of canon law at Ingolstadt University.

Evidently Weishaupt became disenchanted with the Jesuits and the Church in general, for he adopted the teachings of the anti-Christian doctrines of the Manicheans, which he was apparently exposed to in 1771 by a German merchant named Kolmer. (Manicheanism is a religion that was founded in what is now Iran by the prophet Mani. Its dogma is dualistic in nature, putting forth the concept that light and dark are constantly at odds to claim the soul of every individual.) He also embraced the works of radical French philosophers such as Jean-Jacques Rousseau and was considered to be a brilliant young man.

Somewhere along the way, Weishaupt decided that thanks to his training by the Jesuits, he could access power by forming a body of conspirators to free the world from what he perceived as Jesuit domination of the Church in Rome, thus bringing back the pristine faith of the Christian hermetic martyrs. So he founded the "Order of Perfectibilists" or "Perfectionists"—which was quickly changed to "Illuminati" (which he translated as meaning "intellectually inspired")—with five original members.

Weishaupt was said to have no humility or modesty, to possess a huge ego, and to often refrain from using his best judgment in trying to carry out his ambitions. He sought the aid of Freemasons, and although he was successful in gaining entrance to a minor lodge in 1777 and the Illuminati's membership did include some Masons, there's no evidence that he ever gained that group's full support.

I want to emphasize here that many secret societies draw on the Masons' makeup in determining their own structures and often borrow names from Freemasonry for their classifications or levels. And both the Freemasons and Illuminati seem to have been influenced by another secret society—the Knights Templar.

Freemasons, the Knights Templar, and the Rosicrucians have all been linked to the Illuminati by conspiracy theorists, but frankly I haven't been able to find any tangible proof of this. First of all, it's fairly well known that the Illuminati were opposed to the Rosicrucians and their philosophies, so we can eliminate those ties. Second, the Knights Templar were disbanded well before the emergence of the Illuminati. Also, their philosophies were in conflict, so any offshoots of the Templars would be unlikely to join with this group and its New World Order philosophy.

Last, but not least, the Freemasons are picked on a lot by conspiracy theorists. Being the largest and probably most powerful secret society in existence, they've been linked to almost every covert organization that ever existed. While I acknowledge the fact that Adam Weishaupt had a lodge membership, I don't believe his ties went much further than that. Freemasonry was not into the philosophies of the Illuminati and would have rejected their nationalistic plots. I also psychically feel that Freemasonry is a fine organization.

My research indicates that many secret societies get lumped together time after time—in some cases it's legitimate, but mostly these links are either exaggerated or completely false. Of course the Illuminati may very well have tried to infiltrate many of these organizations and in some cases been successful in actually manipulating or controlling them. But their philosophy is too radical to be accepted by religious or fraternal associations, so they're more likely to be adopted by those on "the fringe."

Illuminati members have to swear to obey the organization and their superiors. Members are assigned certain ranks, which fall under three main divisions:

1. "The Nursery" encompasses levels such as "Preparation," "Novice," "Minerval," and "Illuminatus Minor."

2. "Masonry" includes degrees such as "Illuminatus Major" and "Illuminatus Dirigens" (also called "Scotch Knight").

3. The final class, "Mysteries," is divided into both lesser mysteries with the degrees of "Presbyter" and "Regent," and greater mysteries with the degrees of "Magus" and "Rex."

According to author Arkon Daraul, a member in the lower ranks of the Nursery would be very much in the dark as to the way in which the order was run and how it should accomplish its design of "freeing the world." As that person progressed through the various degrees and classes, he'd find out that a significant part of his service to the Illuminati was to gain financial and social power for it. This isn't unlike many secret societies in that the initiates and new members don't have any inkling of what the higher-ups know—in many cases, they're totally unaware of the "true" agendas until they get to advanced levels in the organization.

In his book *New World Order,* William Still states that the famous magician and occultist Cagliostro was initiated into the Illuminati in 1783 in Frankfurt, Germany. Many years later, he reportedly told Catholic priests this about his initiation:

An iron box filled with papers was opened. The introducers took from it a manuscript book [that] on the first page read "We, Grand Masters of the Templars" then followed a form of oath, traced in blood. The book stated that Illuminism was a conspiracy directed against thrones and altars, and that the first blows were to attain France, that after the fall of the French Monarchy, Rome must be attacked.

The Illuminati did expand, and within just 20 years of its founding, this group had gained several thousand members in various countries in Europe. Meanwhile, the conservative ruler of Bavaria and the Catholic Church (with the aid of the Jesuits) were clamping down on Adam Weishaupt and his associates. Soon after the Bavarian government banned all secret societies—including the Illuminati and the Freemasons—in 1784, the organization collapsed in this region, and Weishaupt fled the country.

The Illuminati continued to operate in other areas of Europe, even under the threat of arrest and persecution; and many claim that they finally disbanded in 1790. But other people insist that they still exist today, and my spirit guide Francine agrees. After the group's suppression in Bavaria, it simply became extremely clandestine in its dealings. As several publications with exaggerated accounts of the Illuminati were published after its supposed demise, some historians and conspiracists began to link it to the French and Russian Revolutions, calling it "the ultimate society for conspiracy and revolutionary plots."

In the spring of 1789, for instance, an artificial shortage of grain was believed to have been created by the Illuminati by manipulating the market in France as a ploy to test its theories. The ensuing deficit caused starvation, which in turn sparked rioting in the streets and the storming of the Bastille. Thus began the French Revolution and several years of turmoil for the country. Before Napoleon ultimately took power, the Illuminati gained great headway by manipulating the Jacobites, ultimately obtaining its goals of overthrowing the monarchy and suppressing the influence of the Catholic Church.

The Church was crippled to the point that much of its land was confiscated and many priests were slaughtered. Yet the Illuminati managed this so insidiously that the monarchy wasn't even aware of what was taking place until it was too late. (But Francine says that this is the way complacency sets in—we're so busy surviving that we don't realize that our economy is being eroded . . . like what's happening in the U.S. right now with our gas prices.) The Illuminati felt that this was a great success, which then led to further plots.

From Revolution to Terrorism

As the Illuminati went underground, its members adopted a revolutionary form of philosophy. Although they borrowed different aspects from several other movements, nowhere is their agenda better described than in the "Revolutionary Catechism," which was written around 1873 by a Russian radical named Sergey Nechayev.

Below are a few of the Catechism's edicts, numbered as they are in that text. I chose not to repeat the whole thing here, for I feel that these few examples are quite enough:

> 1. The revolutionary is a doomed man. He has no personal interests, no business affairs, no emotions, no attachments, no property, and no name. Everything in him is wholly absorbed in the single thought and the single passion for revolution.

> 2. The revolutionary knows that in the very depths of his being, not only in words but also in deeds, he has

broken all the bonds which tie him to the social order
and the civilized world with all its laws, moralities, and
customs and with all its generally accepted conven-
tions. He is their implacable enemy and if he continues
to live with them, it is only in order to destroy them
more speedily. . . .

6. Tyrannical toward himself, he must be tyrannical toward others. All the gentle and enervating senti-
ments of kinship, love, friendship, gratitude, and even
honor must be suppressed in him and give place to the
cold and single-minded passion for revolution. For him
there exists only one pleasure, one consolation, one
reward, one satisfaction: the success of the revolution.
Night and day he must have but one thought, one
aim: merciless destruction. Striving cold-bloodily and
indefatigably toward this end, he must be prepared
to destroy himself and to destroy with his own hands
everything that stands in the path of revolution.

7. The nature of the true revolutionary excludes
all sentimentality, romanticism, infatuation, and exal-
tation. All private hatred and revenge must also be
excluded. Revolutionary passion practices at every
moment of the day until it becomes a habit. It is to be
employed with cold calculation. At all times and in all
places the revolutionary must obey, not his personal
impulses, but only those which serve the cause of the
revolution. . . .

13. The revolutionary enters the world of the state,
of the privileged classes, of the so-called civilization,
and he lives in this world only for the purpose of bringing about its speedy and total destruction. He is not a

revolutionary if he has any sympathy for this world. He should not hesitate to destroy any position, any place, or any man in this world. He must hate everyone and everything in it with an equal hatred. All the worse for him if he has any relations with parents, friends, or lovers, he is no longer a revolutionary if he is swayed by these relationships.

14. Aiming at implacable revolution, the revolutionary may and frequently must live within society while pretending to be completely different from what he really is, for he must penetrate everywhere, into all the higher and middle classes, into the houses of commerce, the churches and the palaces of the aristocracy, and into the worlds of the bureaucracy and literature and the military. . . .

18. [There are] a great many brutes in high positions distinguished neither by their cleverness nor their energy, while enjoying riches, influence, power, and high positions by the virtue of their rank. These must be exploited in every possible way; they must be implicated and embroiled in our affairs, their dirty secrets must be ferreted out, and they must be transformed into slaves. Their power, influence, and connections, their wealth and their energy will form an inexhaustible treasure and a precious help in all our undertakings.

19. [There are] ambitious officeholders and liberals of various shades of opinion. The revolutionary must pretend to collaborate with them, blindly following them, while at the same time prying out their secrets until they are completely in his power. They must be

so compromised that there is no way out for them, and
then they can be used to create disorder in the state.

Now aren't these edicts frightening? I also think that
they manifest great evil, to the point that it makes me
wonder what kind of sick person wrote this sort of stuff.
In addition, this all hits home in that it reflects what
many modern-day terrorists believe.

As you can see, the Illuminati's members will go to
great lengths in order to accomplish their goals, and they
put forth much of what society in general is trying to
fight these days: totalitarianism, hate, terrorism, blackmail, and on and on it goes. They don't bend on any of
these premises—everything just becomes more violent
as they become increasingly determined to overthrow
Christianity, governments, social order, and families.

According to many writers, when the Illuminati went
underground, they adopted a variety of names in different
areas of the world. For example, in France they became
"the French Revolutionary Club" and "the Jacobin Club";
in Germany they became known as "the Thule Society";
and in America, they're the group known as "Skull and
Bones" (which was the subject of Chapter 1). And as
recently as 1995, Gabriel Lopez de Rojas founded an order
in Barcelona, Spain, which is said to be directly linked to
the Bavarian Illuminati.

I'm sure that the Illuminati has infiltrated most
political secret societies such as the Council on Foreign
Relations, the Trilateral Commission, and the Bilderberg
Group—as well as the Vatican and various world governments. Francine assures me, however, that although the
organization does still exist today, it's not as powerful as
it once was, so it therefore has a very limited influence.

Nevertheless, we must be ever watchful for New World Order groups; after all, the Illuminati just about succeeded when Hitler and Germany almost won World War II. And in *New World Order,* author William Still states that the Illuminati recently proposed to destroy princes and prelates throughout the world and remove forever the feeling of local nationality from the minds of men and women. The way they'll supposedly do so is by infiltrating high positions of education, administration, press, and politics.

Any group that has diabolical plans that can affect us all will stop at nothing in trying to make them successful. Therefore, it's sometimes better to be a little paranoid so that we don't fall into apathy and wake up some morning under a new government that curtails our freedom. So in this case, I'm in the corner of the conspiracy theorists— and although 75 percent of what they say may be pure speculation, I do worry about the other 25 percent.

The Illuminati far outweighs other secret societies in malevolent intent, and its goal of a New World Order is carried out by numerous organizations that they control or influence. I can say without any prejudice that we're facing pure, unadulterated evil here. We can now see how Hitler was so enthralled with their philosophy. Of all the secret societies I've read about or researched (many of which aren't even included in this book), this one is by far the most vile.

CHAPTER 12

THE "NEW WORLD ORDER"

*A*s I detailed in Part I of this book, the main secret societies in the political arena all have an agenda of a "New World Order," although they may vary somewhat in what they believe that to be. It's certainly not a new concept and can vary depending on who's behind it, but in this chapter I'll just give you an overall interpretation. Prepare to have your eyes opened a bit!

One Government for All?

The New World Order essentially applies to the formation of a global ruling organization that would supersede all individual national governments for the betterment of humankind. In other words, all countries would be run by one system that would control the world's economy, be a peacekeeping entity with its own armed force (with all other armies eliminated), and distribute wealth from rich nations to poor ones so that all on Earth could "have a piece of the pie."

This would be a highly socialistic (some say communistic) way to organize all the peoples of the world—after all, how would you like to have to answer to a planetary government instead of that of your own country? Yet if some covert political groups have their way, it may very well become a reality. In the case of Americans, we'd no longer have a Constitution or Bill of Rights, and we certainly wouldn't have as much freedom. And no matter where you lived, you probably wouldn't be able to carry or own arms, you'd have to adhere to one worldwide monetary system and economy, trade would have little or no constrictions, old laws would be eliminated to make room for new ones (which would then be enforced by a global police force), and peace would be kept by one army.

Religions might not continue as separate entities—in fact, a new worldwide faith would almost certainly come into being. New energy and environmental laws would be enacted; transportation, education, and communication could be controlled by the one government; travel would assuredly be restricted; free enterprise and small business might be eliminated (although I doubt they would be); and all taxes would support everyone in the world by redistributing wealth to poorer nations. Global social services—including health care, retirement benefits, and birth and population control—would be regulated by the ruling organization. I could go on and on, but I think you get the general idea. Instead of individual governments running their own countries, you'd have one entity ruling the entire world.

All right, I can hear you thinking, *Sylvia's lost it.* Yet it seems that countries all over the world have within them key personnel or "plants" from secret societies whose agenda is a New World Order, and their plan seems to start with regionalization. For example, at the State of the World Forum in 1995, Zbigniew Brzezinski (former President Carter's national security advisor) stated, "We cannot leap into world government through one quick step, but rather via progressive regionalization."

If you think that I have in fact gone bonkers, keep in mind that avowed socialist H. G. Wells once fully explained how Western capitalism and Eastern communism would merge into a worldwide government in which, he said, sovereign states (nations) would end and "countless people will hate the New World Order and will die protesting against it." Here are a few more quotes on the subject by some quite famous people:

"The world is governed by very different personages from what is imagined by those who are not behind the scenes."
— Prime Minister Benjamin Disraeli of England (1844)

"Since I entered politics, I have chiefly had men's views confided to me privately. Some of the biggest men in the U.S., in the field of commerce and manufacturing, are afraid of somebody, are afraid of something. They know that there is a power somewhere so organized, so subtle, so watchful, so interlocked, so complete, so pervasive, that they had better not speak above their breath when they speak in condemnation of it."
— President Woodrow Wilson,
from *The New Freedom: A Call for the Emancipation of the Generous Energies of a People* (1913)

*"It will be just as easy for nations to get along
in a republic of the world as it is for us to
get along in a republic of the United States."*
— President Harry Truman (1945)

*"The case for government by elites is irrefutable . . .
government by the people is possible but highly improbable."*
— Senator J. William Fulbright (1963)

*"All of us will ultimately be judged on the effort
we have contributed to building a New World Order."*
— Attorney General Robert Kennedy (1967)

*"In my view the Trilateral Commission represents a
skillful, coordinated effort to seize control and consolidate
the four centers of power: political, monetary, intellectual,
and ecclesiastical. All this is to be done in the interest of
creating a more peaceful, more productive world community.
What the Trilateralists truly intend is the creation of
a worldwide economic power superior to the political
governments of the nation-states involved. They believe
the abundant materialism they propose to create will
overwhelm existing differences. As managers and
creators of the system, they will rule the future."*
— Senator Barry Goldwater,
from *With No Apologies* (1979)

*"Further world progress is now possible only
through the search for a consensus of all mankind,
in movement toward a new world order."*
— President Mikhail Gorbachev
of the Soviet Union (1988)

"We are grateful to The Washington Post,
The New York Times, Time magazine, and other
great publications whose directors have attended our
meetings and respected their promises of discretion for
almost 40 years. It would have been impossible for us to
develop our plan for the world if we had been subjected to
the lights of publicity during those years. But the world is
now more sophisticated and prepared to march toward a
world government. The supranational sovereignty of an
intellectual elite and world bankers is surely preferable to
the national auto-determination practiced in past centuries."
— David Rockefeller,
from a 1991 speech given to the Trilateral Commission
(Source: *The New World Order: Chronology &*
Commentary, by D. L. Cuddy, Ph.D.)

The mainstream media usually ridicules anyone who thinks that there's a plot to create a New World Order. Well, just keep in mind that much of the media is owned or controlled by those who support the concept (see the preceding quote from David Rockefeller)!

Understand that one of the foremost plans of political secret societies is to first regionalize power and then convert it to a worldwide scenario. In recent years, for instance, we've seen this with the formation of the European Union and the acceptance of the euro as the preferred form of currency for most of its member nations. We've seen regionalization in the adoption of the North American Free Trade Agreement (NAFTA) and the creation of the World Trade Organization (WTO). In addition, several countries in South America have already taken the U.S. dollar as their currency, the Soviet Union changed its type of government and economy drastically, and China is becoming more and more capitalistic.

I realize that many will say that I'm making too much out of what may seem like a little, but these are all signs of regionalization and the consolidation of the world's power. I believe that we'll see more of these spreading areas of control in the next ten years, to the point of having different parts of the world utilizing the same monetary system and having "regional blocs of power" come into being. You may think that none of this will ever happen in your lifetime, but even though the changes may seem subtle, as they progress faster and faster you're definitely going to notice signs of a New World Order.

The secret societies that are part of this overall plot for a global ruling body think that the change would be for the betterment of humankind and the world, and many conspiracy theorists feel that it's inevitable. Only God knows what will eventually happen, of course, but despite some assuredly troubling signs, I really don't feel as if any secret society in existence today could ever be powerful enough to have complete planetary domination. There may be several that can wreak havoc and create a lot of chaos, but just like with religion, there's too much diversification in the world's cultures, governments, and countries to have a one-world government. And humankind's survival instincts invariably prevent what would ensure a truly peaceful planet.

Since it's very much like school, the Earth plane was never meant to be entirely blissful . . . after all, it's only temporal. Our *real* Home, the Other Side, is where tranquility and unending happiness reside with the overpowering love of God, making it a true paradise. Just remember that in human life, we'll never be able to duplicate in this reality what our all-loving and perfect God has created for us on the Other Side. It isn't meant to happen here, nor will it.

CHAPTER 13

SCAN

*W*e now come to what I believe is the most secret of societies—it's so far underground, in fact, that no one knows anything about it!

As I stated earlier, many years ago my guide Francine informed our research group about the covert organizations I've covered in this book, including one that she referred to as SCAN. Over the years, however, I haven't been able to find the name *SCAN* anywhere in my vast research (and I do mean vast—at various points my family room has looked like a paper mill blew up in it!).

While writing this book, I found Websites, articles, and entire volumes dedicated to every other secret society mentioned in these pages . . . except SCAN. There's no reference to it anywhere in print, and it seems that even eminent conspiracy theorists don't know that it exists.

Now I'm sure that SCAN, which stands for "Secret Coalition for American Nationalism," is just a generic term for the "overlord" of all the secret societies that are in the process of trying to form a New World Order. However, while the Council on Foreign Relations (CFR), the Trilateral Commission (TC), and the Bilderberg Group

(BG) all think that an organization such as the United Nations is a perfect candidate to oversee the one-world government, SCAN wants everything under American control.

Francine says that because of this, the group comprises 22 people who command and manipulate organizations such as the CFR, TC, BG, and Illuminati, along with some not covered in this book (such as the Club of Rome, Rhodes-Milner Round Table Groups, and the Royal Institute of International Affairs) and every other major and minor covert association and think tank on the planet. SCAN has its fingers in every conceivable pie that carries any influence in the world; in fact, many secret societies were formed by this elite group to be smoke screens for their activities and as a means to attain their goals. SCAN uses such organizations to help control the world's industry, economy, political climate, and social mood. It has no problem with operating in all political systems—be they communist, socialist, fascist, or democratic—and is even involved in the policy making of religions.

Francine did say that although members of SCAN are so powerful that they can regulate economics, world trade, wars, and elections, there's also a spiritual side to them. She explained that if they didn't get too powerful, they could actually bring about a peaceful world order. Personally, I feel that the main danger of an organization like this is that it's so secret that no one other than the select 22 members has any knowledge of how they're going to accomplish their goals. Are they playing special-interest groups against one another, or are they trying to combine these same factions into a viable force for a New World Order? No one knows.

It also bothers me, as I mentioned, that I've never

seen one mention of SCAN in all the research I've done over the years. Since it appears that this organization is so powerful and clandestine that no expert in the field even knows that it exists, I can only hope that it is indeed working for the betterment of humankind.

CHAPTER 14

LIES ABOUT
JESUS CHRIST

*N*ow I'd like to move back to the religious arena, focusing on the biggest secret many of the societies covered in this book have tried to protect—one that revolves around Jesus Christ.

Early Christian sects adopted various forms of Gnostic philosophy, including the concept that Jesus was *not* the son of God or God incarnate, but rather just a Divine messenger. Their reasons for this belief vary, but the main one was that the Messiah didn't die on the cross, but instead lived a very long life on Earth as a husband and father.

In June 1973, my spirit guide Francine stated in a research trance that the Vatican had hidden many books that should be in the Bible, and they were never to be released to the public. This is also what Michael Baigent, the author of *The Jesus Papers* (and co-author of *Holy Blood, Holy Grail* and *The Messianic Legacy*), maintains is true. He theorizes that many of these "gospels" were written at least 30 years after Christ's supposed death.

Francine said that the Christian Bible didn't really settle into its final form for at least 300 years, until the

Council of Nicaea in A.D. 325. Now how many of us could remember everything that happened 30 years after an event, let alone *300* years later—especially if most of it was passed down by oral tradition? Word of mouth is always sketchy because people can put their own spin on a story or elaborate on it to make it more dramatic (or even give themselves more importance).

Anyway, my guide explained that what the Vatican is hiding is proof about Jesus surviving the Crucifixion. I can hear some of you now, saying, "Sylvia, you've gone a little too far this time!" Well, my dear ones, the evidence is piling up. Although it isn't incontrovertible as of yet, I expect that it will become so with new archaeological finds or the discovery of a long-lost document that's been kept hidden for centuries. So let's explore the possibility that this shocking secret that's been covered up for so long might indeed be a fact.

What <u>Really</u> Happened at the Crucifixion

Francine has stated on at least three occasions that Pontius Pilate didn't want Jesus to die on the cross because he didn't feel that Christ was a threat to Rome. Pilate's wife, whom he adored and respected, also had a dream on the eve of the trial that persuaded her to beg her husband not to condemn the young Jew. This, along with Pilate's own belief in Christ's innocence, comes through in the Bible, when the Roman leader asks, "What evil has he done?" and says that "I am innocent of the blood of this righteous man; do as you please" (Matthew 27). This latter statement was made while he washed his hands of the affair.

Michael Baigent has written that Jesus was in favor of the Sanhedrin (the supreme council and tribunal of the Jews) having to pay taxes, which would have endeared him to Pilate and shown that he wasn't a traitor to Rome. Remember that Christ says, "Render to Caesar the things that are Caesar's" (Mark 12:17), which shows that he knew taxes had to be paid.

Francine claims that there was a conspiracy among Pontius Pilate, Jesus, and some of Christ's followers (namely Joseph of Arimathea and perhaps Nichodemus) to have Jesus go through "an execution" that would appear as real as possible. Pilate promised that he'd do whatever he could to make sure that the Messiah wouldn't die. To that end, the Roman leader had the event take place late on the day before the Sabbath (there could be no executions after sunset on this day—and none on the Sabbath itself—and no bodies could be left on the cross after the sun went down). He also made sure that the cross had a footrest and that Christ's legs weren't broken so that he could push himself up to breathe (more on that in a bit).

While Jesus was scourged as was the custom, it was certainly not the way that Mel Gibson portrayed it in *The Passion of the Christ;* in fact, the man was given an opiate to ease his pain. Christ was also pierced in the side (again, as was the custom), but not hard enough to kill him. And Francine says that Joseph of Arimathea, a wealthy merchant, also came prepared to do his part. When Jesus said, "I thirst," he was given a special type of sedative that Joseph had prepared, which knocked him unconscious.

Since Jesus was in a deathlike state, he was taken down from the cross after only a few hours. Most folks took two to three days to die when crucified—even when they used to impale people on stakes in ancient Egypt, it took them many hours and sometimes days to perish. Now I'm sure that what Christ went through was indeed horrendous, but it's hard to believe that a healthy 33-year-old man could have died in three hours.

It's unclear why the Romans didn't then stick Jesus in the ground, where he surely would have died. Instead, Joseph of Arimathea and several others immediately placed him in a rather accessible tomb—it was a hewed-out room of solid rock that stood above the ground, with a stone to cover the entrance—that just happened to belong to Joseph himself.

An often-overlooked nugget of information regarding this comes from France's Rennes-le-Chateau. There's a stained glass window in the Church of the Magdalene there that depicts three men carrying Jesus by his tomb, but the moon is high in the sky. Now since we know that Jesus would never have been buried by someone at night over the Sabbath, this indicates that he wasn't being carried into the tomb, but *out* of it.

Then there's Nichodemus (whom, by the way, Jesus visited during his lifetime). It's been reported in many historical journals that Nichodemus was a healer and could see the future, and he went to Christ's tomb with spices and other accoutrements. Francine reports that these weren't to keep the body from rotting or spoiling, as the Jews weren't into embalming—these substances were intended to revive Jesus.

This is all pure fantasy, you say? Well, let's review some facts. Roman crucifixions ensured torturous deaths by breaking the condemned individuals' legs and keeping footrests off of the crosses. You see, victims with footrests and unbroken legs would be able to push themselves up to a certain degree to relieve pressure on their diaphragms. But this only served to prolong the inevitable, as exhaustion would kick in and they'd eventually suffocate—sometimes after several days. So why was Jesus given the tools for a longer stay on the cross, even though he was put up just a few hours before the Sabbath deadline? The Romans broke the legs of the thieves who were also being crucified, so why didn't they do the same to him?

The piercing of the side of the victim on the cross was to check for death, and as John 19:34 states: "But one of the soldiers pierced [Christ's] side with a spear and immediately blood and water came out." This indicates a few things:

1. There was a buildup of liquid around his heart and lungs (common in crucifixions).

2. Jesus was still alive because of the immediacy of the flow of that liquid.

3. The piercing could very well have helped him survive because it released pressure.

Yet the soldiers declared him dead (learned physicians that they were?), and Christ's body was immediately removed because sunset was approaching.

Now to be fair, Christian scholars say that the rapidity of Jesus's death on the cross was due to trauma, and he'd been scourged so mercilessly that he probably died of heart failure. They point out that he was so weak that he couldn't carry the cross and fell several times on his way to the crucifixion site.

Yes, Jesus was whipped before his trial—but he also appeared before Pilate twice and was sent over to Herod. He presumably walked between all the different courts, so he couldn't possibly have made it if he was scourged to the point that Mel Gibson's film portrays. There's also no proof that the Romans didn't adhere to the Jewish law of "no more than 40 lashes" (Deuteronomy 25:2–3).

In addition, if Pilate was in a conspiracy to save Christ's life, as Francine says, it's doubtful that he would have had him beaten heavily. Even so, the scourging probably did sap his strength (although he was only 33 and strong and healthy). Coupled with not having any sleep during the course of his trial by the Jewish elders, it all probably took its toll. Thus, he fell several times and struggled to carry a cross that weighed 150 pounds or more. Yet that weakness doesn't necessarily explain his supposed quick death. As the Bible points out: "Pilate marveled that he was already dead. So he called the centurion and asked him if he had already died" (Mark 15:44).

Christian scholars might be able to assert that Christ did in fact die on the cross, but their arguments begin to break down when faced with what happened *after* the Crucifixion. If Jesus was resurrected, for example, would there be any reason for the removal of the stone sealing the entrance to his tomb? After all, his resurrected body would be in spirit form and unable to be bound by any human-made structure. Obviously that stone needed to be removed so that his physical body could get out. I know some people would say that someone removed Christ's corpse for safekeeping and then buried it elsewhere. But if Jesus already had a tomb, why put him in another? And the questions about the plausibility of his survival don't stop there.

As we know from scripture, Mary Magdalene is the one who discovers the open tomb (Mark 16:9; John 20:1). She then notifies Peter and John the Beloved of what she's found; they come to verify what she said to them and then depart, leaving Mary sobbing at the tomb by herself. She peers in again and sees two angels, who ask, "Why do you seek the living among the dead?" (Luke 24:5). She explains that she's looking for Jesus so that she can take him away: "They have taken away my Lord, and I do not know where they have laid him" (John 20:14). (Notice that she didn't say "buried.")

Mary Magdalene then sees Jesus but doesn't recognize him. She thinks that he's a gardener, asking him, "My lord, if you are the one who has taken him away, tell me where you have laid him, and I will go and take him away" (John 20:15). The reason that Mary doesn't recognize Christ is fairly obvious: He was in disguise and hiding from the Jews. Second, did this woman really think she could carry a dead man's body? Of course not—she knew that Jesus was alive because she helped take him from the cross!

After Christ calls Mary by her name, she then knows who he is. He goes on to tell her not to touch him, and many Christians believe that this is because he hasn't ascended to his Father in heaven yet. However, those who know that Jesus survived interpret this a bit differently: With his wounds still not healed, he simply didn't want Mary to give him an enthusiastic hug or embrace, which would have caused him pain.

Later on, according to the Gospels, Jesus appears before his apostles to prove that he's still alive. I, for one, can't understand how this can be misinterpreted, but it has been. So let's go through it, starting with Luke

24:36–51 (from George Lamsa's translation from the original Aramaic text; my thoughts are in brackets):

> And while they were discussing these things, Jesus stood among them, and said to them, and they were confused and frightened, for they thought they saw a spirit. *Peace be with you; it is I; do not be afraid.* [Notice here that they thought Christ was a ghost, for they thought him dead.] Jesus said to them, *Why do you tremble? And why do thoughts arise in your hearts? Look at my hands and my feet, that it is I; feel me and understand; for a spirit has no flesh and bones, as you see I have.* [Here we see Jesus trying to explain that he isn't a ghost—as I've explained numerous times, spirits don't carry wounds or have a solid countenance that can be touched and felt, as you or I do. This can only mean one thing: Christ is alive in a real body, not a glorified one.] When he said these things, he showed them his hands and his feet. And as they still did not believe because of their joy, and they were bewildered, he said to them, *Have you anything here to eat?*
>
> They gave him a portion of a broiled fish and of a honeycomb. And he took it and ate before their eyes. [Here again, Jesus shows his apostles that he's alive by eating—yet spirits don't need food!] And he said to them, *These are the words which I spoke to you when I was with you, that everything must be fulfilled which is written in the law of Moses and in the prophets and in the psalms, concerning me.* Then he opened their mind to understand the scriptures.
>
> And he said to them, *Thus it is written, and it was right, that Christ should suffer and rise from the dead on the third day; and that repentance should be preached in his*

name for the forgiveness of sins among all nations; and the beginning will be from Jerusalem. You are witnesses of these things. And I will send upon you the promise of my Father; but remain in the city of Jerusalem until you are clothed with power from on high. [Notice here that Jesus only says he should suffer and rise from the dead to fulfill the prophecies about the Messiah. He doesn't say that he died or is dead, but indeed did go from his tomb and make himself known on the third day. Even though he's alive, he still fulfilled the prophecies as written. It should also be noted here that the fulfillment of the prophecies is mainly one of interpretation—Christians say that he fulfilled them, while Jews say he didn't. In reviewing these predictions, I found most, if not all, of them very obtuse. It seems that Christianity has put its own interpretations on what prophecy is, and it has blatantly misinterpreted many of them as being about the Messiah.]

And he took them out as far as Bethany, and he lifted up his hands and blessed them. And it came to pass, while he blessed them, he parted from them and went up to heaven. [Notice here that it says "he parted from them"—if that was the case, how would they know that he'd gone up to heaven? If Jesus survived, he would have used his common sense and just fled from the land where he could be recognized and per-secuted again on trumped-up charges.]

One of the biggest events portrayed in the scriptures that seems to confirm that Jesus survived the Crucifix-ion is the confrontation with Thomas, related in John 20:24–29:

But Thomas, one of the twelve, who is called the Twin, was not there with them when Jesus came. And the disciples said to him, We have seen our Lord. He said to them, Unless I see in his hands the marks of the nails, and put my fingers in them, and put my hand into his side, I will not believe. Eight days later, the disciples were again indoors, and Thomas with them. Jesus came, when the doors were locked, and stood in their midst, and said to them, *Peace be with you.* Then he said to Thomas, *Put your finger here, and see my hands; and reach out your hand and put it into my side; and be not faithless, but believing.* Thomas answered, saying to him, O my Lord and my God! Jesus said to him, *Now you believe because you have seen me? Blessed are those who have not seen me, and have believed.*

Clearly, Jesus is alive here. Going against the common axiom of Christians that "Christ died and rose on the third day," we see here that it's at least *eight* days before Thomas sees him. Christian scholars will reply that Jesus rose and then went back to visit the apostles, anoint them with the Holy Spirit, and send them out to preach. Yes, he probably did do all of this, but he could very well have been alive for it.

Consider that in the Bible, only the books of Mark and Luke say that Jesus went to heaven, and both apostles are very vague about it—they never confirm that they witnessed his ascension, but rather just assume he did. Also keep in mind that the book of John ends with these words: "There are also a great many other things which Jesus did, which, if they were written one by one, not even this world, I believe, could contain the books that would be written" (John 21:25). Couldn't this be relating to the works performed after his supposed death?

If Christ did indeed survive the Crucifixion (and I believe he did), it would be natural for him to want to keep it a secret. So aside from his disciples, Mary Magdalene, and a few others, he told no one about what had happened. He hid from the Jews and Romans, traveled in disguise to keep from being recognized, and then left Israel for parts of the world in which he wouldn't be so high profile. Many legends and myths describe him visiting the Americas, India, Turkey, France, and England . . . he could very well have done so and continued his work for God.

In *The Jesus Papers,* Michael Baigent reports that he found a wealthy Italian businessman who claimed that he possessed two letters written by Jesus to the Sanhedrin, stating that he was still alive in A.D. 34 and then again in A.D. 45. Baigent said that he'd promised the man who owned the documents that he wouldn't reveal his name to keep him in complete anonymity (which, of course, makes everyone suspicious), but Mr. Baigent did see the letters himself. They were written in Aramaic (the language of Jesus), and he was convinced that they were indeed from Christ.

Now what made this so interesting to me is that 30 years ago, Francine told our research group that Jesus had written sparingly after the Crucifixion, and only to tell the Jewish rabbis that he was still alive. To have it come out as even a supposition in *The Jesus Papers* was overwhelming, as it was a validation of Francine's information. Sure, it may all be a coincidence, but it's certainly a very strong and believable one.

Francine also said that Jesus lived to be close to 90 years of age in France. So as late as A.D. 45, he would have been around 78 years old, assuming that he was 33 at the time of the Crucifixion, as the scriptures recount. So if you do the math, it fits.

The Magdalene Factor

Many Jesuits I've talked to over the years have told me that they believe Christ survived, but they've had to keep it quiet. And as I've expressed many times, I loved Pope John XXIII, especially when he stated that Christ's resurrection from the dead shouldn't be the cornerstone that Christianity is based on. Why would he have said such a thing if he didn't know something about what I've shared with you in this chapter?

Nevertheless, even the notion that Jesus had a family is sacrilege of the highest order to most Christians. Yet just as evidence of his surviving the Crucifixion is coming out, so is proof of his marriage to Mary Magdalene and the children they had together. Here again, such a premise supposedly threatens the very foundation of Christianity, but if something has been built on lies and cover-ups, then it deserves to be torn down.

It's interesting how the Catholic Church initially portrayed Mary Magdalene. Although the early Church probably knew the truth about her, they decided to project an image of her as a harlot in order to further conceal the fact that she was married to Jesus. As most of us know, even though her status as a prostitute was changed and admitted as an error in 1969 by the Second Vatican Council, the stigma is still there.

The Church has always said that the pope is infallible, but here we see a pope (and the Church itself) taking one stance and then changing it later on. The problem I have with this isn't that they admitted a mistake and corrected it—that's laudable. It's that the mistake was made in the first place. How can the Church say that their interpretation of scripture is correct and then admit error? If they erred in this case, what about others?

As an aside, I've always had a problem with religions interpreting holy writings, for they tend to do so for their own advantage. Rebel that I am, I've long been skeptical about taking the Bible literally as a fact-based tome that Christian scholars base their conclusions on. I've found that there are so many inconsistencies and contradictions within these pages that it's absurd.

From a logical viewpoint (and if you just use good old common sense), to take the premise that "if it's in the Bible, it must be fact" borders on the ridiculous. If you study the history of the makeup of the New Testament, for instance, it's almost a joke to assume that it's factual because it's been edited, added to, deleted from, and what have you countless times—not to mention the fact that so many of its books were deemed heretical by the Church. And today, so-called experts admit that they still don't know who wrote the four Gospels, yet we're supposed to accept them as fact! (I wonder if anyone has ever thought that maybe Dan Brown wrote them in a previous incarnation. . . .)

Thank God more and more scholars are taking other writings into consideration, such as the Apocrypha, the Dead Sea Scrolls, and even works from other cultures and religions. New discoveries in archaeology are adding to the mix, and although attempting to piece together our history can often feel like a crapshoot, at least objective scientists are trying to include findings from as many sources as possible.

Getting back to the premise that Jesus was married and had children, many Christians insist that there's no mention of this in the Bible. Here we go again—if it's not in the Bible, then it can't be true. To that end, I simply say, "There are also no writings to say that he *wasn't* a husband and father." In fact, there's definitely more circumstantial evidence to indicate that he actually was wedded to Mary Magdalene. For example, customs of the time didn't recognize a rabbi unless he was married, and books in the Apocrypha mention that he often kissed Mary on the mouth . . . are those the actions of a celibate rabbi who also just happens to be the Messiah?

Mary Magdalene was with Jesus at his Crucifixion, was part of the group that laid him to rest, and took herbs and ointments to the tomb on the morning after the Sabbath to anoint him—even though she would have had no hope of moving that sealing stone. She was the first to find the stone removed and the tomb empty and the first to see him after his supposed death. Some people even view her actions as those of a grieving widow. I don't, because she hadn't actually lost her husband.

I contend that Mary was at the tomb to help heal Jesus with her ointments, and while she knew that it would be open, she was completely surprised to find it empty. As she thought Christ would be inside, her initial reaction was simple: *Where is he? Where has he gone? Who took him?* She knew that he was alive but felt something terrible had happened to him. That's why she didn't run to tell Peter and John that the tomb was open, but rather that he was missing. These actions are completely consistent with those of a worried wife.

Francine says that it was actually Jesus and Mary Magdalene's own wedding at Cana in which he made wine from water. If you read this portion of the Bible over again with the knowledge that it was his responsibility as the bridegroom to provide the wine, it becomes very interesting: "And the master of the banquet [best man?] tasted the water that had been turned into wine. He did not realize where it had come from, though the servants who had drawn the water knew. Then he called the bridegroom aside and said, 'Everyone brings out the choice wine first and then the cheaper wine after the guests have had too much to drink; but you have saved the best till now'" (John 2:1–10). The bridegroom is told that he saved his best wine for last, and who made the wine? Jesus did!

According to the Gospel of Mary Magdalene (which was eliminated from the Bible by the Catholic Church, along with those by Philip and Thomas), she was privy to teachings from Christ that he never gave to the other apostles. This is again consistent with their being married, for they were more intimate and surely had times in which they were alone together for these lessons to take place. The books of the Apocrypha also relate how she was considered the first disciple above all others, again revealing their close relationship and the esteem in which he held her.

Making a Life in France

After Jesus had recovered from his wounds and the ordeal of being crucified, he told his disciples that he was alive and was planning to flee the area. It's only natural to assume that he also filled them in about the plot with Pilate and Joseph of Arimathea and stressed that he needed them to keep his survival secret. He then told them to say that he ascended into heaven and gave them their final instructions to go out in twos to preach to other lands.

Christ then left Israel with his mother, Mary Magdalene, Joseph of Arimathea, and several disciples, and journeyed in disguise up the coast to Tyre. There they boarded a ship and went to Ephesus (in modern-day Turkey), where they stayed for a short time.

Francine says that in Ephesus, Jesus rented a house for his mother to live in and left several of his disciples to watch over her. He then told Joseph of Arimathea to take their ship and go to Britain to establish a base for his new religion there, for Christ knew that he had many mining interests and connections in that area. He told Joseph that he'd reunite with him in Ephesus in three years and that he and Mary Magdalene were going to the Far East.

So, with Joseph off to the British Isles and his mother safely taken care of in Ephesus, Jesus and his wife set off for India with several more disciples accompanying them. They booked passage on caravans for better protection and arrived several months later. Jesus and Mary Magdalene spent many months in India, Kashmir, and what's now known as Pakistan; and according to Francine, they were welcomed everywhere they went. Along the way, they spoke to many who became followers, and these people essentially became the first Gnostic Christians. Rome had little influence in the Far East, so there wasn't much fear of Christ being apprehended, but he did need to check on his mother and meet Joseph of Arimathea.

Joseph had spent a very productive three years away from Jesus. Francine says that not only did he maintain his mining interests, but he also made many converts and started to build a church in Glastonbury, England (which is said to be the oldest above-ground Christian church in the world). In addition, Joseph was able to explore the nearby country of France—so when he and Jesus met again in Ephesus, it was he who suggested that France would be a good place for the couple to make their home.

Thus, Mary Magdalene and Jesus picked up his mother and the other disciples and set sail for France. They landed near Marseille and went a bit inland, eventually settling close to the Rennes-le-Chateau area in the Languedoc region. Francine says that Mary Magdalene had already given birth to their first child, a girl named Sarah, by the time they arrived. She also states that they spent many years in southern France and actually had seven children, of which only four survived.

According to Francine, the local people in the area became very protective and kept all of the Holy Family's secrets very well (including that Jesus was from Judaic royalty, descended from David, and that Mary Magdalene came from a wealthy family that also had ties to royalty). Jesus, Mary, and their children weren't threatened in any way, and they were safely hidden away by their neighbors when any danger did happen to appear on the horizon.

As time went on, Mary Magdalene became really active in preaching and teaching. While Jesus would give the occasional sermon and do infrequent healings, he mainly confined himself to instructing children and writing. (This probably was done to lessen notoriety and fame and to keep his location a secret more than anything else.) Jesus did take a trip or two to Britain with Joseph, but these were very low-key. Mary, on the other hand, traveled in a wider circle and consequently became much revered in the whole of southern France.

My spirit guide claims that Jesus lived until he was in his mid-80s, and Mary Magdalene died some 20 years later, when she was in her mid-90s. As Christ's mother had died about ten years after they settled in France, all three were buried in that country. The presence of the Holy Family did have the impact of making the south of France a Gnostic stronghold over the years. Both the Knights Templar and the Cathars had great influence in the area, and the Catholic Church had a very difficult time establishing a strong presence there for centuries.

Secrets Have Led to Lies

Now maybe it's because my ministers and I have known this information for so long, but we're certainly not blown away by any of the revelations in this chapter. What I don't understand is why any of this would disturb the Divinity of Christ. After all, Buddha and Mohammed weren't sacrificed, nor were any of the other messengers that God has sent to humankind, and it hasn't affected *their* Divinity. Since I'm a Gnostic Christian, I feel that Jesus was the greatest of "the direct reporters" from God, but that doesn't mean I don't pay homage to Mohammed, Buddha, the Dalai Lama, or even the Bab from the Baha'i faith. If you look closely, you'll see that they all have the same basic message of loving God, doing good, living simply, and remembering that this world is a plane of learning to give homage to our Creator. Even modern-day psychics and prophets (at least the good ones) profess that what they get comes from God. As long as they don't let their egos and greed get into it, they're going to keep their channels pure. (Of course by no means do I intend to put any of us—especially me—on the same level as

God's direct reporters.)

I know that many Christians believe in the concept of Jesus dying for our sins (the Atonement), but it was Paul who came up with this, not the man from Nazareth. Others might insist that Christ's survival affects the whole concept of resurrection—but almost everyone is resurrected back to the Other Side after death! I guess having a son of God who supposedly died and came back to life (like no one else has been known to do, except when Jesus himself brought Lazarus back from the dead) puts Christians in the position of believing that their Messiah is head and shoulders above any other messenger.

What these people seem to forget is that Christ's marvelous works, teachings, and healings had already proven him to be a miracle worker and an icon in his own time. And his real success was in bringing us the truth about our all-knowing and all-loving God, Who was nothing like the violent, vengeful Creator of the Old Testament—and this had very little to do with his Crucifixion or Resurrection. How ironic it is that many Christians choose to emphasize Christ's death and rebirth, thus failing to recognize all he did while he was alive.

So if Jesus didn't die on the cross, does that take away his Divinity? Of course not! He was absolutely a Divine messenger and his teachings still survive . . . and we must remember that he thought such teachings were the most important part of his mission for God.

≈

I'll no doubt be ostracized by fundamentalist Christians for putting out the truth about Christ living beyond his crucifixion, although I simply can't understand how his marriage, kids, and long life make him less of a Messiah. The early Catholic Church evidently thought they did, though, for it created a massive cover-up that's still perpetuated to this day.

The Church has painted itself into a corner with all of its suppression; and indeed, there would be earth-shaking ramifications in the whole Christian world if the facts ever become common knowledge (which I predict will happen someday). In fact, so much has already come out in new discoveries and will continue to do so, despite religions trying to suppress it. The facts are there for those who want to research them, but humankind's troubling penchant for apathy—along with an unbeliev-able religious attitude of rejecting truth even when it's indisputable (such as with many Protestant faiths)—will keep them in the Dark Ages.

Unfortunately, many Christians will have to continue to wallow in their self-made world of ignorance and prejudice, blindly following so-called leaders who continually preach very dangerous concepts such as guilt and fear. These zealots prey on those who truly believe in their dogmas of a fearful and vengeful God, even as they fill their coffers with ill-gotten gains.

Churches just keep emphasizing that we need to be afraid of God and repent for our sins. Wake up, people! God is merciful, forgiving, and loving. He knows the plane of existence we're in and all its temptations, so He understands that all of us will transgress in varying degrees. Since Jesus forgave all those who were pure of heart, wouldn't our Creator do the same? Christ is the Messiah for those of us who believe in an all-loving God; for those of you who think that God is to be feared, look elsewhere for your savior, for he isn't Jesus Christ.

If you'd like to read more about what I've brought up in this chapter, I suggest beginning with *Holy Blood, Holy*

Grail, which was the first mainstream work to say that Christ wasn't executed by the Romans. While some of the research from that book has proven to be suspect, its main premise remains true; and I commend the authors for their daring because they got others to search further into the enigmas they described.

Then came books such as *The Dark Side of Christian History* by Helen Ellerbe; *The Woman with the Alabaster Jar: Mary Magdalene and the Holy Grail* by Margaret Starbird; *The Gnostic Gospels* and *Beyond Belief: The Secret Gospel of Thomas* by Elaine Pagels; *Misquoting Jesus: The Story Behind Who Changed the Bible and Why* by Bart D. Ehrman; and, of course, *The Da Vinci Code* by Dan Brown. I highly recommend all of these works, and remind you to think for yourself on this (and any) subject.

CHAPTER 15

≈

SUPPRESSION OF THE GNOSTICS

*B*efore we delve into this chapter, I'd like to give you some background about Gnosticism. Many historians say that the belief stemmed from Zoroastrianism, which was founded by the ancient Iranian prophet Zoroaster, whom scholars believe lived sometime between 1000 and 1400 B.C. Zoroastrianism is perhaps the first religion to put forth the concept of angels, and a summary of its tenets would be: "Good thoughts, good words, and good deeds." As it was one of humankind's earliest organized faiths, it had great influence on many that came after it, such as Buddhism, Islam, Manicheanism, and Mandaeanism.

Mandaeanism is interesting because its adherents (who are still practicing today but only number around 50,000 to 75,000) don't believe in Buddha, Jesus, or Mohammed, but they *do* have a great reverence for John the Baptist. In fact, all of these early Gnostic religions claimed a connection to various biblical figures, yet they tended to differ greatly about whom they recognized.

Ancient Gnostics also felt that there were two forces in creation: a good god and a bad one (or what we in

177

modern times might call "the devil"). The good god was basically unreachable, but the bad one created the earth plane and all of its evil and temptations. This is known as "dualism," and if you do any research on Gnosticism, you'll run across this term frequently. (It also signifies light and dark and good and evil.) In fact, all of the early Gnostic religions, such as Zoroastrianism, Mandaeanism, and Manicheanism, believed in the concept of dualism.

Modern-day Gnosticism differs greatly from the ancient sects, especially when it aligns with Christianity, as is the case with my church, the Society of Novus Spiritus. For example, while we recognize that Jesus Christ was a special and Divine creation from God and His messenger, we also believe that we are *all* sons and daughters of God—that is, Jesus wasn't the only one.

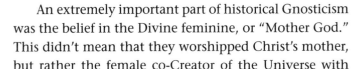

An extremely important part of historical Gnosticism was the belief in the Divine feminine, or "Mother God." This didn't mean that they worshipped Christ's mother, but rather the female co-Creator of the Universe with "Father God."

Naturally this whole philosophy was heretical as far as the Catholic Church was concerned, so it was kept underground. But if we, as the Bible states, were made in the image and likeness of God, then we can only assume that there's a duality in our Creator, just as there is in humankind and all of nature. In ancient times, most of society deemed the male superior to the female because of his physical strength. This, of course, is no longer the case; nevertheless, it's still more convenient to have a patriarchal religious society.

Yet as I've written in other books (particularly *Mother God*), the vast majority of human beings believed in the Mother God or Goddess before the time of Christianity, including people living in various powerhouse empires such as the Romans, Babylonians, Egyptians, Phoenicians, Persians, Turks, and Greeks. And since vanquished nations invariably accepted the religions of their conquerors, the Mother Goddess came to be worshipped by almost everyone in ancient times. So it wasn't until Christianity became widespread, during the time of Roman emperor Constantine, that suppression of the feminine principle gained steam—which actually had more to do with Christian factions than the emperor.

You see, since Constantine was Roman, he already worshipped the Mother God, but the empire was in decline and the Christians were creating a lot of trouble for him. So Constantine negotiated with Christian leaders and came up with the Edict of Milan, which granted religious freedom. He became a Christian himself and was the head of the church as well as emperor of the land. Also, since Romans devoted a day of worship to their sun god, Apollo, Constantine designated Sunday to be a day of rest. (Interestingly enough, Constantine is recognized as a saint by the Eastern Orthodox Church but not by the Roman Catholic Church.)

The Emergence of Pauline Christianity

When Constantine issued the Edict of Milan, he probably thought that the infighting within Christianity would cease, but it didn't. After several years of constant bickering among various early sects over interpretations of dogma, he evidently got fed up and called the Council of Nicaea in A.D. 325 to end conflict once and for all (it didn't, but he made a valiant effort). At the council, the emperor laid down the law and forced the various hierarchies of the early Christian Church to agree to some uniformity and to set up a better infrastructure for the purpose of stabilization.

The battle among these factions during Constantine's reign ultimately resulted in a showdown between Pauline and Jewish Christians. As their name suggests, the Paulines followed the teachings of the self-proclaimed apostle Paul, and they fought for members with the Jewish Christians who followed the teachings of James and John the Baptist. (Paulines are also called "gentile Christians" because they didn't tend to have Jewish ancestors.) These two factions were in conflict with each other not only over doctrine, but especially over how Paul had interpreted the life of Jesus and his teachings on what kind of person Jesus was.

Jewish Christians, who were mainly comprised of those with Jewish ancestry, also included Christ's relatives (who purportedly belonged to the Ebionite sect). They didn't embrace the ideas of the Messiah's Divinity or his "virgin birth"—in other words, while they felt that Jesus was a great messenger and followed his teachings, they didn't believe him to be God incarnate. Isn't it interesting that members of Christ's own family didn't consider him to be Divine?

The Paulines won over Constantine, which is why so much of Christianity is apostolic (following the teachings of the apostles) in nature. In fact, the parts of the Bible that are almost always used in Christian theology classes are not the Old Testament and very rarely the four Gospels, but are instead the epistles of Paul.

Here again we must realize that Paul never actually met Jesus. However, he *was* one of the few in his time who could write, so he made up his own publicity and claimed to know all about the great teacher. If you've seen Martin Scorsese's movie *The Last Temptation of Christ* (which is banned by the Catholic Church and very controversial for a number of reasons, including a scene of Jesus having sex with Mary Magdalene), you may remember the part when Paul addresses Christ on the cross and remarks that he can make anything he wants out of Jesus. Even though it's Hollywood, there's a great amount of truth in that statement—that's why I say we have more "Pauline" Christians than "pure" ones.

One could go so far as to make the case that Paul has influenced Christianity more than Jesus has. You see, as I mentioned in the last chapter, most Christians have been brainwashed into thinking that the Crucifixion and Resurrection were the most important things, which is what Paul continually emphasized.

Paul is at odds with Jesus here, for Christ's whole intention was to bring the "new law" of an all-loving God to the people. Many forget that Jesus was a Jew and remained one throughout his life, staying loyal to the religion of his birth but offering new and greater interpretations of the scriptures, which ultimately turned into the teachings of Christianity. (Does anyone realize that Jesus wasn't Christian—after all, what did he do, follow himself?) He shared the beliefs of his relatives, who were essentially Jewish Christians. Now since Paulines opposed these individuals, the Christianity of today is actually in direct opposition to the teachings of Jesus. Ironic, don't you think?

The Church's Grip Tightens

As the Paulines gained power and influence, their persecution of other sects began to rise. Since Jewish Christians were so secular and only interested in staying in Israel, they were no real threat and more or less faded away. However, they did share the secret of Christ's survival of his Crucifixion with the Gnostics.

This group tried to exact changes in the Pauline (Catholic) Church, mostly to no avail. Gnostics also attempted to fight the rising corruption within the Church, but they were simply outgunned. It became more and more apparent that the Church was gaining power, wealth, and influence due in large part to corruption, all of which was only going to be used against the Gnostics. Thus, they did what they had to do in order to stay inconspicuous, holding their secrets tightly to themselves, away from the outside world.

It was during this time that the Church began to run roughshod, bullying its followers by telling them how to worship and live and backing it up with various forms of manipulation and fear. Catholic leaders controlled entire countries under the guise of religion, and they employed fear tactics—including the threat of excommunication and hell for those who failed to cooperate.

These years made the Catholic Church a world power, yet one whose history was tainted with blood and corruption. Murder and assassinations became frequent as rival hierarchies tried to gain power, and indulgences became commonplace. And there was often more than one pope, as different factions tried to rule at the same time. These "anitpopes," or those individuals whose authentic claim to the papacy was questioned, appeared frequently from the 3rd century until the 12th, and again in the 14th and 15th centuries. This just underscores how corrupt and political the Church was during these times—almost 40 times in their history, even they couldn't decide who the legitimate pope was!

～

Since society in medieval times consisted solely of the poor masses and the elite, there was no middle class. The upper class consisted of members of the Church and the noble aristocracy, while the majority of people were condemned to serfdom—mainly farmers and trades-people who worked for the few in power. Oh, you had some merchants thrown in there, too, but because communication and travel was so limited, those individuals tended to confine themselves to local areas for both their wares and their customers, so they very rarely had much money.

Except for Catholic leaders, most people were also highly uneducated. Even the aristocracy of the time was illiterate, so the Church gained even more power because it was looked upon as being a learned institution. Lands were either owned or controlled by the Church or the nobles, and the subsequent taxes they charged to the masses kept them wealthy.

During this period, the Gnostics were very secretive and were content to worship out of the sight of the ever-growing and powerful Church. Yet suppression of the masses was what eventually led to Gnosticism regaining some influence. Life was so harsh and religion so strict that the general public started looking elsewhere for spiritual sustenance, which many people found in Gnostic sects.

At this time, nobles were continually warring with each other—while they manned their armies with knights mounted upon steeds, they used the poor as foot soldiers and cannon fodder. The Church was embroiled in all of this as well, making alliances with the most powerful of the nobles and lending money to others to finance their battles in return for land, autonomy, and power.

Consequently, many kings became mere lackeys for the Church and had to do whatever it told them to. Other members of the elite became disenchanted with Catholicism's power and started giving sanctuary to Gnostic sects, especially in the south of France. Protected by local nobles, these Gnostics began to gain influence as they sought favor with the general populace. Perhaps the most influential group at this time was the Cathars, a Gnostic Christian sect that was truly pious and dedicated to poverty. They became so popular in the south of France that they actually threatened the Catholic Church's hold on that area for a time.

The Cathars

The Cathars are certainly an enigmatic bunch, seeming to weave in and out of the path of the Knights Templar and other groups. They're even difficult to research because most of what we know about them comes from the writings of their enemies. I don't think this is because of historians' neglect, but rather by the Cathars' design. I agree with my spirit guide Francine, who states that this group tried very hard to stay pious and private.

According to historians, the group adopted its name around the middle of the 12th century, and the word

Cathar is thought to have originated from the Greek term for "pure ones." This sect seems to have its roots in druids, alchemists, mystics, and early Gnostics; in fact, scholars believe that it evolved from the Gnostic teachings of western Europe and possibly had ties to Manicheanism. The Cathars were also known as "the Albigensians," supposedly because of the chronicler Geoffroy du Breuil of Vigeois. In 1181, he referred to the town of Albi in southern France as being the area they came from.

As I explained in the last chapter, the south of France has been the source of myths about Jesus and his family for centuries. Now if these stories aren't true, why would they continue to have such strength? It's also interesting that many Knights Templar lived in this area—southern France has certainly been a hotbed of Gnostic activity. (Of course at that point, the area wasn't yet a part of France but instead, what's now known as Spain. You must remember that it was a time of kingdoms, fiefdoms, and duchies that were scattered all over Europe—in other words, countries' boundaries weren't like today's clear-cut borders.)

Like the Knights Templar, the Cathars have a legend in their history that claims they were the keepers of a fabulous treasure. Some say it was none other than the Holy Grail, while other believe it was ancient scrolls of knowledge, and yet another group maintains that it was a sacramental sword in a carved wooden box. Whatever the treasure was, it was supposedly taken by four Cathar monks out of their castle of Montsegur, just a day or so before the stronghold fell during the Albigensian Crusade. The monks then slipped through the armies of the Catholics and escaped to some hidden place, never to be heard from again.

Francine confirms that the treasure was indeed taken out of Montsegur just before its fall and that it consisted of sacred teachings, including information about the bloodline of Christ and his life in France after the Crucifixion. There were no jewels or the like because the Cathars didn't ascribe value to worldly goods, other than for sustenance or to help the poor.

The nonviolent Cathars made many friends and converts, since the harsh life of medieval times and the constant political squabbles between nobles had made things very tough for the lower classes. Throw in the Catholic Church, which wanted to control everything spiritually and ruled with an iron fist, and you have a fallow field that was ready to be planted with a new crop of ideas.

When the Cathars migrated into what is now southern France, in the Languedoc region, they probably had no idea how successful they'd be. They entered this environment and found a willing audience for their new ways of doing things. They brought with them a type of freedom and solace that hadn't been seen for as long as the poor masses could remember. Finally someone was attending to people's needs without asking anything in return—no tithes or indulgences. There was no taking up of arms to fight some stupid war, and no working from dawn to dusk to help feed an army that was out who knows where.

The Cathar theologians, or "perfecti," were also known as *bons hommes, bonnes femmes,* or *bons chretiens*— "good men," "good women," or "good Christians." Their followers were named "credentes" and were purportedly not initiated into the doctrine at all; instead, if they agreed to receive what was called the "consolamentum" (the baptism of the spirit) before their death, they would be freed from all moral prohibition and religious obligation.

The Cathars impressed people with their teachings. Their acceptance of life with all its faults and frailties prevented them from condemning anyone; consequently, no moral prohibitions or rules were ever put forth (as the Church had done). Interestingly, this had a profound effect on the masses: Instead of running around and partying all the time, they became gentler, kinder, and more helpful to their friends and neighbors. It was almost psychological trickery in that they could raise hell if they wanted to with no punishment, so it wasn't fun to break the rules anymore. While many loved to challenge Catholic dogma as a rebellious act, the Cathars had no such restrictions and were so kind that many soon found that there was nothing to rail against.

This Gnostic group was kind and peace loving and attended to the poor by providing them with an education, setting up hospices, and otherwise taking care of them. Cathars lived frugally, had no strict rules, held services in the open forests and fields, and seemed to genuinely care about people. In addition, women were put on an even plane with men, and priests gave spiritual counseling and performed services in homes if necessary.

In contrast, the bishops representing the Catholic Church were corrupt hypocrites, charged money for sacraments, seemed aloof and uncaring, and demanded the strict observance of a multitude of harsh rules. It's no wonder that the Cathars established a firm foothold in Languedoc, so much so that Catholic cathedrals were frequented less and less. Thus, the Church deemed the Cathars to be heretics—regardless of the fact that their followers were receiving much-needed solace and help.

The reigning religious authorities had always dealt vigorously with those whom they considered to be heretical, which heretofore had been composed of small groups who weren't considered to be any real problem. The Cathars, however, were a different matter. By converting Catholics and thus lowering the Church's revenue in the area, these Gnostics were becoming a real threat . . . and as usual, the Church had a response. But before we get into that, let's first explore the beliefs of the Cathars in greater depth to find out why the populace was so attracted to them.

Cathar Beliefs

The Cathars believed that within every person existed a Divine light or spirit (most commonly known today as the soul), which was trapped in a world of temptation and corruption. As Gnostics, they believed in dualism, or that this world was created by a lesser deity who proclaimed himself to be the one and only Creator (much like Satan). The Cathars then put forth that orthodox Christianity also believed in a false god and that the Catholic Church was a corrupt abomination that was deeply influenced by the prison of earthly life's materialism. Spirit, the vital essence of humanity, was therefore trapped in a negative physical realm that was created by a false god and ruled over by his demoralized minions.

To free yourself from this jail of the human condition, the Cathars believed you had to first become aware of the evil and depravity that existed in the reality of human life—which included the ecclesiastical, dogmatic, and social structures of that time. Once you were cognizant of the "prison of matter" and its corruption, then you could set about breaking its bonds, which was a step-by-step progression that was different for each individual. Becoming kinder, gentler, more spiritual, less materialistically oriented, and freeing oneself from addictions were just some of the ways to set the spirit free.

The Cathars accepted the world as it was and consequently learned to transcend it. They taught that in order to go beyond this earthly life, you had to experience it. You couldn't run away from the world, but if you genuinely experienced all it had to offer, both positive and negative, at that point you could throw off the shackles of addictions and attachments. In other words, all of the temptations of life, including the last vestiges of holding on to pain and loss, had to be extinguished before you could begin to transcend. When you were no longer bound to the world, then you could truly enjoy it.

The Cathars believed in reincarnation but never saw it as a necessary or desirable process. Rather, they realized that some individuals wouldn't be able to free their souls from the earthly prison in only one lifetime, so they recognized that it might take some people more existences to attain their freedom.

This group also completely rejected the Old Testament and embraced the Gospel of John as their most sacred text. In it, Christ states, "A new commandment I give unto you; that you love God with all your heart and soul and mind, and that you love your neighbor as yourself." With this one simple statement, the Cathars eschewed the rules, regulations, dogma, indulgences, and penances of the Catholic Church. To these Gnostics, loving God and one another was all that was necessary in the spiritual journey. They understood that simply living in this way would help set them free from this "prison of life."

Cathars believed that Jesus Christ was a pure manifestation of spirit who wasn't constrained by the limitations of matter and that he was the messenger of the true God of love, which the faith embraced. They pointed out that the false god of the Old Testament demanded fearful obedience and worship from his "children," and if he didn't get it, the result was often torment and murder. The dogma of the Trinity and the sacrament of the Eucharist were also rejected by the Cathars, as was purgatory, for they believed that life on Earth was punishment enough.

Members of this sect took their beliefs beyond the religious, although most of them directly related to the jail of the human condition. For example, they believed that giving oaths was wrong because it only tied one more to the dominion of the world. This certainly flew in the face of the medieval period, since most business transactions and allegiance to nobles and the like were carried out with oaths due to the level of illiteracy.

Sexual abstinence was also preached by the Cathars, even in marriage, as they felt it freed them from "slavery to the flesh." Perfecti were expected to practice complete celibacy, often leaving their spouses when they reached that level to lessen the temptation of "senseless intercourse" that continued to imprison those who practiced it. And the destruction of life in any form also went against their beliefs, so perfecti wouldn't eat any creature except fish, or any by-product of animal reproduction (cheese, eggs, milk, butter, and the like). But interestingly enough, the perfecti didn't condemn any of their followers for having sexual intercourse or eating foods tied to reproduction—they just required these choices of themselves and any who wanted to reach that stage.

As I related before, the followers of the Cathars were freed of any moral prohibitions. Although the perfecti certainly preached their beliefs, they led more by the example of their own holiness, which endeared them to the masses. And while the perfecti lived ascetic lives with respect to food, clothing, and celibacy, they maintained an elegance in their simplicity. They wore simple cloaks and didn't have anything like hair shirts or beggars' clothing. Everyone they met, regardless of station, was treated the same—from the poorest of serfs to the richest of nobles. And when compared to Catholic monks and bishops, the Cathar perfecti seemed gentler, kinder, more pious, more honest, and much more moral—not to mention that they led exemplary lives as they educated and helped the unfortunate. Consequently, people flocked to them in droves.

A Most Terrible End

With the "good people" making such inroads into converting Catholics, it was inevitable that something would eventually be done about them. Some say that it began with a political move by the king of France to capture the southern area to enlarge his kingdom, while others claim it was just the Church exerting its power once again to suppress any perceived threat. Francine says it was a little bit of both: The Church needed an army to fight its battle, which the French king provided, but only if the Church allowed him to keep the conquered land. Much of this had been brewing for a long time, as the nobles of the southern region were quite adamant about not being taken over by France. And since medieval times were very political and the Church had its fingers in almost everything, both the Catholic leaders and the king of France were able to come to an agreement.

The growing influence of the Cathars ultimately led to several significant historical events:

1. It sparked another Crusade by the Catholic Church, this time with the goal of wiping the Cathars from the face of the earth. Called the Albigensian Crusade, the ensuing violence was extreme—even by medieval standards.

2. The Church got its mercenaries to offer conquered lands to the king of France and northern French nobles, which would eventually nearly double the size of that country.

3. The Church had a role in the creation of the Dominican Order, which was founded to "preach the gospel and combat heresy."

4. The Church created and institutionalized the truly horrible Inquisitions, of which the Spanish is the most infamous.

Speaking of the Inquisitions, millions of women were killed and tortured because they were thought to be witches and "working in league with the devil." Now why didn't anyone realize that getting rid of all of the women would cause the population to suffer? This isn't surprising, though, since from its inception the Catholic Church has always been patriarchal in nature: It demands celibacy from its priests so that they won't have to support families, women aren't allowed to serve in the priesthood, and church dogma dictates that women be obedient to men.

～

In 1198, Pope Innocent III came to power determined to rid Languedoc of the Cathars. At first he tried peaceful means, such as having his priests in the region try to convert the Gnostic group, but he met with little success. In 1204 he then suspended the authority of the bishops in southern France and appointed papal legates to oversee the situation. Again there was little progress, so the pope sought support from the nobles in the region and excommunicated those who didn't cooperate.

The powerful count Raymond VI of Toulouse refused to act against the Cathars and was excommunicated in 1207. After a heated argument between the count and a papal legate sometime in 1208, that papal legate mysteriously died. Upon hearing this, Pope Innocent issued a papal bull to start a Crusade against the Albigensians (Cathars) by offering the land of the heretics to any who would fight. Many in northern France took up the offer, and soon it was north against south.

The fighting in the Albigensian Crusade went very well for the pope and the northern armies between 1209 and 1215. Then there was a series of revolts and reverses between 1216 and 1225 in which almost all the lands seized were taken back. France's king, Louis VIII, finally intervened in 1226. He proceeded to take charge and wiped out the last Cathar stronghold of Montsegur in 1244. About 15 years before that time, however, Pope Gregory IX instituted the first Inquisition to rid the area of heretics.

The estimates of Cathars killed even before the formation of that Inquisition is close to 200,000, yet it's unclear whether or not that number includes those who defended the group. For example, in July 1209, the papal legate Arnaud-Amaury surrounded the town of Béziers, France, with his army and demanded that the Cathars be turned over to him. The town of nearly 20,000 refused, even though there were only about 500 Cathars hidden there. When the legate was asked how to distinguish Cathars from the citizens of the town by another crusader, Arnaud-Amaury is said to have answered, "Kill them all! God will know his own!" Somewhere between 10,000 and 20,000 people were slaughtered that day, most of whom weren't even Cathars, according to an eyewitness, writer Caesar of Heisterbach.

Then a ruthless course was started in 1233, as Cathars were burned wherever they were found and dead bodies were even exhumed for that purpose. Having taken religious vows against hurting or killing anyone, the perfecti had been unable to protect themselves, but throughout the Crusade, thousands of people had risen to their defense, including many people of different faiths. After a ten-month siege in which 200 Cathar perfecti and 300 soldiers held off 10,000 crusaders, the Church's soldiers found a breach in the defenses and the "good people" could no longer be protected.

Although the last known burning of a Cathar by the Inquisition wasn't until 1321, for all intents and purposes the Cathars fell at their stronghold of Montsegur and were essentially wiped out. While a few monks did manage to slip away with their "treasure," the remaining perfecti gathered with their supporters and were marched down in front of the castle and put into a huge pyre. It's said that while they were burning, they left their lives singing a hymn of praise to the true God of Love. In any case, I'm sure that they found their "kingdom not of this world," as Jesus always said.

Putting the Focus Back on Jesus

The interesting thing about religious secret societies is that almost all of them were Gnostic in nature. That's because they had to be—not only because of the information they protected, but because it flew in the face of the establishment. Gnostics have tried throughout the centuries to rise up and give back the truth about a loving Father *and* Mother God, along with Christ's survival and lineage; and each time they've been called heretics and ostracized, persecuted, and killed.

Yet information is coming out fast and furious these days. I personally have no fewer than 50 books that confirm what I've related in these pages, much of which Francine reported decades ago. This isn't my ego speaking here; it's more to let you know that not everyone goes into trance or hears their guides, as I do. After reading my books (that I know were infused by Spirit), people by the thousands have let me know that "what you said [or wrote about] rang true in my soul" or "I always felt this way but couldn't express it—or if I *did* try to tell anyone, I worried that I'd be called crazy." Well, I believe that the universal truth resides in every human being and resonates deeply. This especially applies to Jesus—his words were so simple and true that they begin to feel as if they were etched upon our very souls.

I've always believed that Jesus was Gnostic because he

was an Essene, which was one of several schismatic sects in the Judaic faith. The Essenes' primary base was Qumran, where the Dead Sea Scrolls were found. But in the book *The Templar Papers,* compiled and edited by Oddvar Olsen, there's a chapter written by Sandy Hamblett (the editor and publisher of *The Journal of the Rennes Alchemist*) that expounds on recent archaeological evidence that shows the Essenes lived on Jerusalem's Mount Zion at the time of Christ. You may wonder what the significance of this is. Well, Mount Zion was purportedly the location of the Last Supper, along with being the headquarters of the Knights Templar more than a thousand years later!

Further evidence comes from the discovery of the "Essene Gate." You see, there were many gates to Jerusalem, all of which were named after directions to either areas in that city or places beyond the gates. (For example, "the Damascus Gate" led to the city of Damascus.) The archaeological discovery of the Essene Gate was made from the remains of an ancient wall that had once surrounded Mount Zion, and the Essenes were known to surround themselves with such barriers to keep out the general populace. In fact, Jesus was said to have moved freely in the walled-in community of these Gnostics.

Archaeologist and Dominican priest Bargil Pixner also found the remains of ritual baths exactly like those found in Qumran, and the Essenes were noted for their rituals of cleanliness and purity. When Pixner presented his evidence to a noted Israeli archaeologist, he replied, "Here you have excellent proof that the Essenes lived in this quarter of Jerusalem."

It's also interesting to note that in these early days, the Jewish Christians were accepted to the point that they were allowed to build a church in Jerusalem. Now where do you think that church was located? You guessed it—on Mount Zion. Called "the Church of the Apostles," it was erected on the same site that had been razed by the Romans in the first Jewish revolt in A.D. 67–68 and where the Last Supper was held in an Essene synagogue.

Based on his research, famed archaeologist Yigael Yadin put forth a theory that Christ led a schismatic inner sect of Essenes. Now it's known that John the Baptist was a prophetic leader, an Essene, and a cousin of Jesus—so did Jesus take over John's leadership after his death? Many think so. It's also known that John the Baptist sent some of his disciples to join Christ's group—one of whom was John the Beloved. From there, according to Sandy Hamblett, "We move into Gnostic theology and the theology of the Gospel of John."

A thousand or so years later, the Knights Templar (who were often called "Johaninne Christians" and "the Knights of St. John") came on the scene, and many theorize that they protected Christ's descendants. Thus, we have the whole mystery of the Merovingian line and of these early Jewish Christian sects evolving into Gnostic Christians such as the Cathars.

Now why would the so-called secrets that the Gnostics possessed induce such a flurry of hate, wars, and rebellion? Well, we have to look at how powerful the Catholic Church was in influence and wealth. If you didn't follow its dogmatic rules, you were told that you'd go to hell. This type of attitude fostered the practice of indulgences (that also augmented the coffers of the Church), which was mainly people paying the Church to absolve their dead or dying relatives of sin so that they'd stay out of hell.

The Church finally righted itself after the Reformation led by Martin Luther, and after the formation of the

Anglican Church in England gave it a big wake-up call. However, as Catholics and Protestants fought over who would rule the Western world's Christian population, both factions put Jesus on the back burner.

Both faiths took on Paul's interpretation of Christ's life and teachings, turning him into the son of God who was crucified and then resurrected. In no way could they accept that our Lord was married or had children, for in their minds that would keep him from being Divine. And if Jesus didn't perish on the cross, there's no way to give guilt to all of those who were told that "he died for our sins," and there would be no premise of the Resurrection. So this led to the severe editing of the Bible, including the expurgation of many Gospels. *Everything* had to conform to the Pauline view.

Gnostics, on the other hand, revered Christ's teachings but believed that he was just a messenger from God. They knew that he was married and had children, didn't die on the cross, had a human side, and couldn't be called "God." They also believed in the duality of a Father and Mother God and put forth the concept that you could worship Them anywhere and that Their kingdom resided in your soul.

When the Cathars and Knights Templar tried to promote these messages of truth, they were exterminated by the Christians. That's because such teachings only promise love, forgiveness, and solace to humankind, without the fear of retribution. This, of course, keeps members out of church, and the big business of "saving souls" is negated. So to evade persecution, underground Gnostic groups began to form in the hopes of surviving long enough to let people know the real mission of Christ.

The Truth Keeps Coming Out . . .

The next secret that I'm about to relate may not necessarily seem to have anything to do with the theme of this book, but as you read on, you'll see how well it fits.

It's amazing how synchronistic life is—so many times when I'm working on a project, people will come up with off-the-wall information about the very subject I'm writing about, without my ever mentioning it. As I am completing this book, it's happening again. In the last two days, programs have been appearing all over TV relating to a new discovery of Gnostic writings that were found in the 1970s and sequestered away by the National Geographic Society. It seems that they had four to six scholars putting together more than 1,000 pieces of ancient papyrus for study and translation before they felt ready to make the material available to the public. That discovery was the Gospel of Judas.

Now what makes this frighteningly accurate is that my guide Francine has championed Judas for years, and I'm sure it dismayed many people that she wouldn't back down about it. I'd even bring it up in my lectures, saying that Judas had to do what he did in order to carry out the plot of Christ's so-called death on the cross. I've also used him as an example of what happens when we're too quick to judge others.

In May 1972, our early research group (most of whom are still around today) were avidly interacting with Francine during a trance. She'd been talking about the life of Jesus when someone asked about Judas. The transcript of the session verifies that she specifically states, "He has been vilified so wrongly over all these centuries—he actually was a very important pawn to fulfill the conspiracy that went on between Pilate and Christ, but they had to make [the Crucifixion] look real to make the Sanhedrin believe it was authentic. He had to go and give Jesus up as a dissident. Christ himself begged him to do it, although Judas didn't want to." She went on to say that Jesus convinced him to play this role because no one else could be trusted to do so. So Judas took on the role of the traitor and has been branded as such ever since.

The reason I've inserted this here is because this is part and parcel of the secret knowledge that the Gnostics carried. A few of my ministers have said, "We should have been the first to bring this out," but I told them that it wasn't the right time. In the 1970s, the world was not ready to hear this information, as spiritual awareness was only in its infant stages, and everyone was just following the rules. Not until the '80s did people start questioning things more—and even then my group and I were looked at askance, as many individuals didn't know whether we were delusional or just plain crazy.

As the Bible says, there's a time for everything. Yes, we were aware of this information long before it was released to the public, but so what? My philosophy has always been that I don't care who brings forth the truth, as long as it makes people think and then react. As I've said a million times, listen, research, read, think, and then take with you what feels right and leave the rest behind.

I think it's simply wonderful that centuries' worth of hidden information is finally being brought to light. When I asked a question in school, I never believed the response that "there is no answer because it's a mystery." Now I know from Francine that for any question we can think to ask, there's a logical explanation from God. Why give us inquisitive minds if we're not supposed to know the truth?

Why are any of the secrets that the Essenes, Templars, Cathars, and other Gnostics knew so controversial? They certainly don't disturb the Divinity or messages of Christ, so what makes them so earthshaking? Jesus always tried to explain his ideas to his followers in ways that they would understand. He spoke in parables to the uneducated masses so that they would better comprehend what he was trying to teach them. He never couched his words in mysticism or cryptic concepts and never answered questions by saying, "It's a mystery," unlike many religious organizations today.

If anyone has been to my lectures or read my writings, I'm constantly explaining that Gnostics try to stay true to Christ's words, whether in the Bible or in other texts such as the Apocrypha, and refrain from their own private interpretations. Yet it's apparent that almost all Christian churches do their own readings for their own needs. That takes us to the final chapter in this book, in which I explain how much corruption and conspiracy can result when the truth is twisted or suppressed.

CHAPTER 16

CONSPIRACY THEORIES
AND CORRUPTION

*S*o many covert organizations, fraternal groups, and even religions start out with the best of intentions, only to become tainted by certain individuals' egos and agendas. While Jesus preached that the earth is not our kingdom, many folks perform activities for their own personal gain . . . even as they tell themselves that they're building a better world. Somehow, these people are convinced that cover-ups and atrocities are "necessary evils" for the betterment of humankind in general.

Many governments on this planet work in the same way; in fact, it's not that much of a stretch to say that they're secret societies, too. After all, we only know what our leaders tell us or what's unearthed by some investigative reporter. Don't get me wrong—the United States is the freest nation I've ever seen, but we have to wonder how long that's going to last. Sure, we have the Freedom of Information Act, but I'll bet that 95 percent of my fellow Americans don't even know what it is . . . and even if it's utilized, only the tip of the iceberg can be accessed.

We citizens really know very little about the clandestine operations our government conducts every day.

I mean, how many of us realize exactly what the CIA does or has done in the past? I'm not saying that this organization is evil, since I'm sure that many of their actions are for "homeland security" and the protection of our nation, but they *have* committed some horrible acts over the years.

For example, the CIA, FBI, and related groups have been known to set up dictators all over the world, who then turned around and committed genocide. So when does morality come into play? When will someone draw the line to stop these types of occurrences, especially when they further the interests of our own country?

I know that this is going to sound like George Orwell's *1984*, but when you stop and think about it, how much freedom do we really have? Even today, people all over the world are being persecuted because of their ethnicity, race, gender, sexual orientation, and religion. Those in power can create wars; lobby bills into law; regulate our gas, electricity, and food; and control what we do and say. If even Americans can have our IRS forms sold, identities stolen, conversations recorded, and rights curtailed in myriad areas, what can the average person do?

Well, we can go on with our lives and do the best we can. We must keep our friends and loved ones close and pray that none of them ever gets caught up in addictions, crime, or occult groups. I have quiet faith in the human spirit—especially spirituality itself. Just remember—particularly as you read these next several pages—that while this is a dark planet, that doesn't mean we can't let our own lights glow.

A Warning from Francine

As I've said in my lectures and TV appearances, as a lot of our religious dogma breaks down, covert and often-times occult groups will be on the rise. The formation of such associations are generally the direct result of men and women feeling somewhat lost and then focusing upon their base human wants. While these people may be attracted to the secret societies that are spiritual or political in nature, there are other communities out there that may appeal to them. These organizations appear to be so bizarre and insane in their activities (such as drinking blood, sacrifices, and so forth) that they're what I call the "fringe societies."

My spirit guide Francine says that many of the founders of these groups are definitely "dark entities." Such individuals allowed their egos to override their intellects as they tried to gain power in any way they could, thus causing a separation from God. Dark entities want to win over this planet—which will never happen because "white entities" (which is what most people in the world are) will never turn dark. However, many white entities do join fringe societies and cults, be it out of ignorance, the search for spirituality, or as a response to a charismatic leader.

For example, most of the unfortunate people who died in Jim Jones's cult were white entities who were just looking for a messiah. Of course Jones himself was dark, enamored as he was with his own greed and self-importance. You may wonder why the white entities couldn't see through this . . . well, a lot of them did. Unfortunately, by that time they were stuck in Guyana with no way out. I'm sure that many of them just drank the Kool-Aid to escape the hopeless and helpless feeling of being browbeaten and brainwashed by a madman.

Nor can we assume that every person who followed Adolf Hitler was as dark as he was. So many of these men and women were caught up in the dictator's charisma, idolizing him because he brought back pride in Germany after its defeat in World War I. When power corrupted him and led to so many unspeakable acts, many of these followers feared for their own lives. Yet the white entities who initially revered him ended up fighting against him.

Francine confirms that "any white entity can be manipulated, but eventually snaps back on track like a rubber band." She goes on to say, "There is probably no one in this world who hasn't in some way been manipulated by dark forces because of the negative vibration of this planet." She then warns that many founders of secret societies prey on the false ego and fears of human beings. (In other words, you're told that you'll gain entrance to heaven or some other sort of a reward by following them.) They're also usually amoral and will express that it's all right to profit at the expense of others.

My spirit guide reports that some of these clandestine organizations are manipulating many of the world's affairs already, causing epidemics (AIDS in Africa?), problems with the food supply (mad cow disease?), energy crises (brownouts and gas shortages?), and war (the Middle East, Vietnam, Korea, and Bosnia?). She continues by saying that if you think these things are frightening, they're just small pinches before the "big squeeze" comes.

In answer to the inevitable question of "What do we do?" I'm reminded of what Francine told my research group three decades ago:

Your spiritual essence will rise up, and you will go on a Gnostic search to find what our Lord said: to find your own spiritual truth that is not only within you, but outside. This in itself fights the battle against negativity. As insane as everything will become at the turn of the century [keep in mind that she said this in the 1970s], the more sanity will fight valiantly to overcome it.

Remember that the schematic for this planet's reincarnation pattern is almost at an end. So because too many entities want to finish up, they're coming in tired and shell-shocked—they haven't had enough time to gather enough spiritual strength and essence, so they're like lemmings running to the sea.

Francine truly was a voice crying out in the wilderness, and what amazes me are her prophecies about world events so many years before they happened. For example, she discussed germ warfare, saying that there would be many strange diseases and afflictions arising in the next few decades. Well, are we not seeing this come to fruition with the emergence of fibromyalgia, chronic fatigue syndrome, the Epstein-Barr virus, Legionnaires' disease, SARS, and the avian flu? She also said that multiple sclerosis and Lou Gehrig's Disease (or ALS) would be increasing, that Alzheimer's disease would run rampant, and that more and more children would be affected by ADD (attention deficit disorder) and ADHD (attention deficit/hyperactivity disorder).

I'm still on the fence about so-called attention disorders because I don't think they exist, and too many individuals who definitely don't have the conditions are diagnosed with them. It seems that if people don't fit into some preordained category, we give them a label to separate them from the "normal" human experience and then call them outcasts or shun them completely. Is this any different from Hitler's attempt to create a pure Aryan race? Human imperfection has always been met with fear and bigotry.

The Secrecy and Lies of the Vatican

If we're going to discuss conspiracy theories and corruption, we certainly can't ignore the Catholic Church. To that end, I'd like to briefly look at Pope Boniface VIII. Boniface was elected pope in 1294 after the abdication of Pope Celestine V—and one of his first acts was to imprison Celestine until the former pope died in 1296 at the age of 81. Boniface would later become known for formalizing the jubilees, for issuing his famous bull *Unam Sanctam* in 1302, and for his involvement in "temporal" affairs that caused enmity between the Church and several rulers, especially King Philip IV ("Philip the Fair") of France.

Boniface made some of the boldest claims for the spiritual supremacy of the papacy, proclaiming: "It is necessary for salvation that every living creature be under submission to the Roman pontiff." He was constantly at odds with King Philip IV, who was taxing the Church heavily to pay for his wars. Boniface excommunicated Philip in 1303, which ultimately led to his capture and detainment by the king.

As you can see, Pope Boniface VIII was nothing if not strong in both his dealings with others and in his opinions. Many in the Church didn't love him, but instead feared him, especially since he's reported to have said the following (although some scholars dispute this):

- "The Christian religion is a human invention like the faith of the Jews and the Arabs."

- "The dead will rise just as little as my horse, which died yesterday."

- "Mary, when she bore Christ, was just as little a virgin as my own mother when she gave birth to me."

- "Sex and the satisfaction of natural drives is as little a sin as hand washing."

- "Paradise and hell only exist on earth; the healthy, rich, and happy people live in the earthly paradise; the poor and the sick are in the earthly hell."

- "The world will exist forever, only we do not."

- "Any religion and especially Christianity does not only contain some truth, but also many errors. The long list of Christian un-truth includes the Trinity, the Virgin Birth, the godly nature of Jesus, the Eucharistic transformation of bread and wine into the body of Christ, and the resurrection of the dead."

Strong stuff . . . and it provides food for thought on the perceived outlook of Christianity and whether or not it has been built on lies and deception. After all, these statements were purportedly made by a pope who was privy to what his religion knew.

Francine says that if we could just get into the private archives of the Vatican, then we'd see the truth. I mean, if the Catholic Church isn't hiding anything, why can't we get into these archives and do research? Even though some areas have been opened up for scholars lately, access has certainly been controlled. I find it funny that when famous author Taylor Caldwell agreed to go under hypnotic regression for Jess Stearn's book *The Search for a Soul: Taylor Caldwell's Psychic Lives,* her guide Darios brought back so much information that the Vatican contacted Caldwell to ask who'd been spying inside of its walls for her. I guess if you've based your beliefs on years of secrecy, then you'd naturally be suspicious.

I can only conclude that the Church feels that the truth will hurt or even destroy them. Otherwise, why don't they come forward with all the knowledge they have, which could shed light on the findings that have recently emerged about Jesus, Mary Magdalene, the Dead Sea Scrolls, and the Nag Hammadi writings? I'm sure that most of the hierarchy of the Church isn't even aware of what exists in its deep caverns of aging manuscripts, so we must try to refrain from being too judgmental. However, we can continue to ask questions about the information it has long suppressed.

～

The Catholic Church has spent much of its existence in a state of internal turmoil, and as its history dictates, it was a great source of cruelty and fear. Its Crusades and Inquisitions killed millions, as did the constant zeal for wealth, control, and power. For centuries, the Church's intention always stayed the same: to subjugate the poor while calling for war and change in the name of God.

Even the Renaissance period brought no great relief to the poor, although the arts and sciences were starting to flourish. Instead of numerous tiny fiefdoms existing, powerful countries such as England, France, and Spain started to take shape; but the warfare continued, as did the Church's political ambitions and lust for power.

At this time, more secret societies sprang up than ever before. Some were after wealth and power through a New World Order, while others (such as the Cathars) just wanted the right to worship God in their own way. It's interesting to note that the underground groups that sought religious freedom were for the most part destroyed, while those that pursued power, wealth, and control are still around today. This plane of existence on Earth is truly a place where evil abounds and thrives—which in no small way is due to humankind's thirst for power and wealth, especially when it comes to the world's faiths. Now, to be fair, the Catholic Church of medieval times was much different from the Church today, but don't we still see religion everywhere wreaking havoc—albeit in a slightly more subtle manner?

Personally Speaking . . .

I know that I sound like the worst enemy of the Catholic Church, but I assure you I'm not; in fact, all this negative information only makes me heartsick. I wanted to be a nun and loved the 18 years I spent as a Catholic-school teacher, but I had no choice but to tell the truth as I saw it. If what I've found had been about the Baptist, Mormon, or Episcopalian faiths, it would have been the same thing. I'm nothing if not honest, and all of the information I've shared with you in these pages is in the history books for anyone to see.

Being a former Catholic (and still a little bit of one in my heart), I sometimes mourn what the Church might have been, but I can't ignore the atrocities, murders, corruption, and so on that it has performed in its long and troubled history. I just wish that the "big boys" of the Vatican would be more honest. I've made friends with many nuns and priests over the years, and I know firsthand that these wonderful people selflessly try to help as many individuals as they can every day, while the power brokers spend their time covering up scandals. It makes me want to cry.

Since so much of my life was spent in service to the Church, I know for a fact that the good priests and nuns I worked alongside were just as ignorant as I was . . . except I never stopped asking questions. I was always put in the principal's or dean's office during my Catholic education, often being assured that "it's all a mystery," that I had no right to delve into what didn't concern me because I was female, and that I was awfully egotistical to think I could come close to knowing what the great theologians did. This would keep me quiet for a time, and then off I'd go again.

The fact that the Church is so patriarchal doesn't sit well with me. By no means am I an activist for women's liberation, but I do believe that we should be on an even plane with men. The Church, of course, doesn't see it that way.

I'll never forget Father Freeman, who came to talk to the all-girls' college of St. Teresa (now known as Avila University) that I attended in Kansas City, Missouri. He went off on a tirade about the defects of women and how they should keep their "place" (whatever that was). I listened to this speech for about an hour until I couldn't stand it anymore. I raised my hand, even as I saw my college administrator, Sister Regina, turn red. I asked him, "Father, with all due respect, how would you have arrived on this Earth without a woman giving birth to you? Whether good or bad, you still got here by what had to be God's ordained way for us to enter this planet."

He was silent for a moment and then replied, "What is your name?"

"Sylvia Shoemaker."

"Well, Miss Shoemaker," he said, "you've had your say, and I've had mine." And with that, he exited the stage.

The other girls attending the lecture cheered, and I hesitantly walked by Sister Regina, who looked me right in the eyes and smiled. I can tell you that was when I finally noticed how hard my heart was pounding.

The reason I share this story is because even in my college days in the 1950s, we were educated in what were thought to be "acceptable" careers for women—namely, teaching and nursing. Or we could be "good home-makers" and raise a family while being nice, obedient Christian wives.

Nevertheless, I argued constantly with nuns and priests—poor things, I'm sure they were thrilled when I graduated. Although just the other day I was talking to one of my former principals, whom I've always loved and admired, and I apologized for giving everyone such a hard time. To my surprise, she replied, "Don't be silly! We loved you and knew about your search for spirituality and truth. Besides, you kept us on our toes so that we'd read and research." This certainly made me feel so much better than to look back and see myself as an aggravating rabble-rouser.

Another interesting thing happened during my college days when a Jesuit friend of mine named Father Thomas told me, "You know, Sylvia, we were all talking this morning around breakfast and out of the blue, someone just said, 'What if we [the Church] turn out to be the anti-Christ?'"

I was appalled by this statement, and by no means am I inserting it here because I believe it. Rather, I just wanted to show that the Jesuits can be very philosophical about things, even addressing subjects that conflict with Catholic dogma. I guess that's why I have such an affinity for them—I've always loved the rebels.

The Jesuits are envied a bit by some members of the Church because they're considered to be a very elite order. Many of them hold high positions in the Church's hierarchy because they're the faith's teachers and researchers, and many of them have founded great universities. I remember that in my college theology classes, there were often brief statements or allusions to the Jesuits being the renegades of the Church because many felt they knew too much, which meant that they couldn't be controlled.

I recall a teacher of mine, Father Hicks (not a Jesuit), once remarking that the Jesuits had been almost excommunicated at one point. When I asked him about the statement the next day, he stammered and said, "S-sometimes I talk off the top of my head." I think that the Jesuits' reputation comes from their information about Church history, which, of course, would include the Gnostic influence. Knowledge brings power in many ways, especially when most people don't have access to the same material. And I'm so intrigued that out of all the orders that were available, the Jesuits chose to absorb the Priory of Sion.

Anyway, after Father Thomas brought up the possibility of the Catholic Church being the anti-Christ, it took me a few minutes to calm down. Finally, I asked my friend what in God's name provoked what I felt was such a blasphemous statement at the time (1954). He replied, "Oh, I don't know . . . maybe I'm just down and have been doing too much historical research on the Church and reading about different groups."

Not until years later did this response give me chills. I have to tell you that the more I find out about the Catholic Church, the more upsetting it becomes, especially if you've been as close to it as I have. Again, I'm sure that the majority of Catholics don't know any of this and never even had any provocation to look for something that they're not even aware exists.

The Problem with Organized Religion

Christianity, especially Catholicism, has probably the bloodiest history of any major religion in the history of humankind. In 1998, Pope John Paul II even went so far as to apologize for the Catholic Church's lack of action against the Nazis in World War II. In March 2000, he again expressed remorse, this time for the Crusades, the persecution of Jews, and the unjust killing of heretics. Both times, however, he maintained that it was only certain Catholics and not the Church itself that had committed these wrongs. He named no names, but admitted that these members of the Church had erred in their judgment.

Unfortunately, these statements received very little publicity, which was of no consequence to those who feel that the Church can't say that it's sorry enough. Today many people are seeking new apologies, especially in light of how some Catholic priests and nuns have been involved in sexual scandals with the molestation of young people. It just goes to show how exceedingly slow the Church is to admit error, but how can it really apologize for all that it's done over the centuries? At least to the institution's credit, it did finally acknowledge some wrongdoing, which relieves some of the hypocrisy, but certainly not the harm done. Those corrupt individuals within its ranks must live with what they've done every day.

I can muster up a little sympathy for the modern Catholic Church, which tries to downplay its history and cover-ups . . . what else can it do? It has had its path dictated by its corrupt forefathers, and I don't see its course changing until it's forced to do so. The recent scandals and its unbending conservatism are only adding to its decline, for it has definitely lost power in this world. In fact, the Church's karma seems to have caught up with it, thanks to a lot of bad press and the fact that it's had to pay out millions in lawsuits because of the sex scandals.

I'm sure that if the Catholic Church wasn't so wealthy and powerful, all of this negativity would have finally brought it crashing down, but you're talking about an organization that goes back hundreds of years and has its fingers in business, banking, and commerce, as well as many covert activities. It must be so hard for the devoted priests who know the truth yet must practice under that umbrella of deceit.

I really don't mean to single out Catholicism here, as it really is a gentler and more loving religion now. Unfortunately, I see conservative and evangelistic churches of all faiths springing up left and right these days, spouting hate and bigotry and using the fear of hell and God to control their flocks and to tell them how to live.

When Christians look at Islam and wonder how extremist clerics can send their faithful followers out to kill others and themselves while putting forth messages of hate against the infidels, *I* wonder how Christian pastors and ministers can spew out their animosity toward homosexuals, minorities, or anyone who doesn't believe the way they do. Unless both faiths start preaching and enforcing the Golden Rule rather than spreading messages of hate and bigotry, they're nothing but hypocrites.

Many religions start out with good intentions and then become corrupted by leaders' quests for money and control. When wealth and power become more important than God, it's time to move on. And if someone quotes scripture to you and then says "But what it really means is this," look out!

I believe that regardless of who or where you are, you can love and worship God. You can join a religious organization with its tenets and dogma, but it's imperative that you feel free to really love God. Any group that tells you how to live, what to eat, or how to act while using the threat of guilt, sin, and excommunication is an occult organization. Unfortunately, that label applies to many of the world's faiths, as they've actually become secret societies that suppress information.

My guide Francine says that no religion is the only one to carry truth—there's virtue in all of them, but they have different ways of paying homage to God. Yet if the faiths of Islam, Judaism, and Christianity continue to massacre each other both in words and deeds, they're truly perpetuating evil and hypocrisy, and we'll never get out of the "dark ages of religion." All three must start to reverse their course and teach tolerance, kindness, and a love for their fellow human beings.

God made us all equal, and as everyone has his or her own personal relationship with God, who can say whether one is better than another? Belief and faith are intrinsically your own, like perhaps nothing else in this world is. So since you only know the breadth and depth of your own belief, you must only speak for yourself.

In other words, we can't judge others' beliefs, nor can we come to conclusions about them based on their closeness to God. We can only gauge how close *we* are to Him. Also, if our all-loving Creator is perfect and omnipotent, then there's no way that he could ever be evil, vengeful, or wrathful. Humankind has attributed natural disasters, disease, and all our other woes to Him. In addition, we're taught to fear Him and not reciprocate the love that He gives to us.

I personally condemn those who think that God doesn't love all creatures in His creation—to think that He wouldn't love a certain race or ethnic group is stupidity in action. To say that God is on anyone's "side" during a war or genocide that's supposedly in His name is completely illogical and wrong; instead, we're actually insulting Him, for we're destroying His work. Anyone who truly loves God will always be against human beings' cruelty toward each other.

We must defend ourselves against the world's atrocities by continuing to shine our lights, always with the hope that someday those who commit heinous actions will realize that their own agendas—be they personal or for a group or nation—*must* take a backseat to God for us to ever have peace in this world. If we're tolerant of each other and watchful of the occult organizations, such negativity will disappear—after all, these societies won't be able to operate without devoted followers and financial support.

AFTERWORD

t's been fascinating for me to go through all the information that has come out about covert organizations, conspiracies and corruption, the New World Order, and various religious and political cover-ups and scandals. However, trying to ferret out the links between all the groups, as well as separate the truth from myths and false claims, also occasionally led to a big headache.

I certainly opened a can of worms when I chose to write a book on secret societies, since many of the topic's scholars, researchers, and theorists have their own agendas, be it the Catholic scholar trying to defend his religion or the fanatic who insists that extraterrestrials have infiltrated every gathering. It can also be disheartening to realize that many in these associations seem to be "puppet masters"—orchestrating wars, influencing the economy, or controlling our natural resources—and we may feel as if Big Brother is truly watching us. Although they protest that they're not occult in nature, these groups seem to be quite virulent in their practices. My logic is, if you're doing the right and moral thing, why do you need to cover it up?

My guide Francine says that we won't be ruled by these clandestine organizations in our lifetime, but as time goes by, they *will* gain in power and numbers. By no means do I think that rioting or other acts of dissension are the answer—rather, as simplistic as it seems, love and spirituality *will* conquer all. That doesn't mean that we should turn a blind eye to the corruption and conspiracy that's so prevalent in our world; instead, we must walk through the darkness and give hope and love wherever we can, just as Jesus did.

Money and power have become the new gods for so many, but when we maintain or increase our own spirituality, we remain the beacons of light that can never be snuffed out. We must also realize our own failings, for as Jesus said, "The best of men fall seven times a day." It's when we're so busy trying not to sin that we can find we're not being ourselves. And when we're not ourselves, we can never truly live freely and happily, shining for all the world to see.

In times of adversity, I always petition Mother God because She is the one, we might say, Who can make miracles in our lives as well as create a type of harmonic convergence in the world and all its insanity. So if you really get in trouble, pray and petition to Her to get results. (For more on this, please see my book *Mother God*.)

~~~

I'm afraid that there will always be underground groups, but hopefully the negative ones will lose their potency thanks to all of the literature out there now. If you join a society or religion, just be watchful and remember that if it doesn't feel good, it probably isn't right for you. Like Jesus said, go and find your own temple—that is, the one that God gave you and you live in—and meditate about it. Your gut will tell you what's right and wrong for you, so you don't need to follow the path of others if it doesn't feel good inside.

Secret societies have been with us from the beginning of written history (and Francine says that they were around even before then). I think that's because on a spiritual, emotional, and social level, humankind has always wanted to feel special. And as far back as prehistoric times, we banded together against the elements or predators.

We humans have also always come together to fight oppression and hardship, no matter the time or place. For example, my father grew up in the northeast section of Kansas City, Missouri. Even before the Depression, everyone there was poor; and the Jews, Italians, and Irish pulled together to make it. Yet as time has gone on, the planet has become more segregated, bigoted, and paranoid. It's not necessarily our fault, as the wars, terrorists, murderers, rapists, and kidnappers we see on the news every day all contribute to a jaundiced view of life.

Today, gangs band together as warriors. They have leaders and what they feel is a purpose, even if it's only to defend their "turf." Many might call it a negative bonding, but to them it's probably the closest connection of their lives. You see, gangs usually form in disadvantaged and poor neighborhoods that have lots of crime, broken families, and alcohol and drug abuse; and although the members tend to come together for mutual protection, they're often the only family each other has. I'm convinced that the breakdown in our beliefs and political systems, as well as in our family and community life, is what has caused gangs to proliferate. Nevertheless, they do exist and are a prime example of people banding together for survival.

It's human nature to find a place where we can belong and feel important. But it's vitally important that we get together spiritually and help each other, too. As Francine reminds us, "Your purpose in this life is to lose self and to give of yourself. Most of you coming into this period of time probably found that it was harder for you to give of yourself because of the confusion in this world, but hopefully through your search for spirituality, you have been able to be more affectionate in giving of self.

"This is a process that is learned, especially in this time of discord, war, and turmoil—so you may have a tendency to pull in and become isolated. If you don't watch it, you can develop this isolation and form an austerity about you. This means that out of fear, loving qualities can go begging. This doesn't just mean that you must always physically embrace, but there is a spiritual, psychic embrace." I have to break in here to say that the physical embrace can be wonderful, too—I love when I'm at a book signing and someone asks, "Sylvia, can I just hug you?"

Anyway, my guide continues, "It's easy; you take a broad spectrum of humanity and love them. You can be discerning, but loving others does bring the good toward you. Dark entities, unless they want something, are repelled by unconditional love."

When someone asked Francine what we can do in the hopelessness of this negative world, she replied, "Well, it's really in the essence of what you strive for to find yourself and your God within and the God without. Don't let yourself be manipulated by power or mysticism, and fight the battle against negativity."

So again the rules to follow are simple. Don't listen to anyone who puts him- or herself above everyone else. Make sure that the rules and regulations don't take away your freedom to search and seek your own God center; then take your freedom to worship and love God in your own way. Francine used to say that if you put three or four people in a room, you can have a mini-universe, with different experiences and views. But in my 70 years, I've found that humans have an enduring need not only to belong, but to follow a universal truth that seems to work for all of us.

As I end this book, I'd like you to keep these words from my spirit guide in mind: "You must understand that even if just one of you goes out of here and begins to light other lights, you have made a place of darkness turn bright."

I truly wish each and every one of you strength and courage as you illuminate the world.

God love you. I do,
Sylvia

About the Author

Sylvia Browne is the #1 *New York Times* best-selling author and world-famous psychic medium who appears regularly on *The Montel Williams Show* and *Larry King Live,* as well as making countless other media and public appearances. With her down-to-earth personality and great sense of humor, Sylvia thrills audiences on her lecture tours and still has time to write numerous immensely popular books. She has a master's degree in English literature and plans to write as long as she can hold a pen.

Sylvia is the president of the Sylvia Browne Corporation; and is the founder of her church, the Society of Novus Spiritus, located in Campbell, California. Please contact her at: **www.sylvia.org**, or call **(408) 379-7070** for further information about her work.

29 June 2011

WEDNESDAY
evening
10 PAST 8 PM

We hope you enjoyed this Hay House book.
If you would like to receive a free catalogue featuring additional
Hay House books and products, or if you would like information
about the Hay Foundation, please contact:

Hay House UK Ltd
292B Kensal Rd • London W10 5BE
Tel: (44) 20 8962 1230; Fax: (44) 20 8962 1239
www.hayhouse.co.uk

✳✳✳

Published and distributed in the United States of America by:
Hay House, Inc. • PO Box 5100 • Carlsbad, CA 92018-5100
Tel.: (1) 760 431 7695 or (1) 800 654 5126;
Fax: (1) 760 431 6948 or (1) 800 650 5115
www.hayhouse.com

Published and distributed in Australia by:
Hay House Australia Ltd • 18/36 Ralph St • Alexandria NSW 2015
Tel.: (61) 2 9669 4299; Fax: (61) 2 9669 4144
www.hayhouse.com.au

Published and distributed in the Republic of South Africa by:
Hay House SA (Pty) Ltd • PO Box 990 • Witkoppen 2068
Tel./Fax: (27) 11 467 8904 • www.hayhouse.co.za

Published and distributed in India by:
Hay House Publishers India • Muskaan Complex • Plot No.3
B-2 • Vasant Kunj • New Delhi – 110 070.
Tel.: (91) 11 41761620; Fax: (91) 11 41761630.
www.hayhouse.co.in

Distributed in Canada by:
Raincoast • 9050 Shaughnessy St • Vancouver, BC V6P 6E5
Tel.: (1) 604 323 7100; Fax: (1) 604 323 2600

✳✳✳

Sign up via the Hay House UK website to receive the Hay House
online newsletter and stay informed about what's going on with
your favourite authors. You'll receive bimonthly announcements
about discounts and offers, special events, product highlights,
free excerpts, giveaways, and more!
www.hayhouse.co.uk